THE PAULINE LETTERS

INTERPRETING BIBLICAL TEXTS

INTERPRETING **ibt** BIBLICAL TEXTS

The Pauline Letters

Leander E. Keck & Victor Paul Furnish

LLOYD R. BAILEY, SR.
and
VICTOR P. FURNISH, EDITORS

ABINGDON PRESS   NASHVILLE

THE PAULINE LETTERS

Copyright © 1984 by Abingdon Press

Library of Congress Cataloging in Publication Data

KECK, LEANDER E.
The Pauline letters.
(Interpreting Biblical texts)
1. Bible. N. T. Epistles of Paul—Hermeneutics.
I. Furnish, Victor Paul. II. Title. III. Series.
BS2650.2.K43   1984   227'.06'01   84-6171

ISBN 0-687-30494-6

MANUFACTURED BY THE PARTHENON PRESS AT
NASHVILLE, TENNESSEE, UNITED STATES OF AMERICA

INTERPRETING BIBLICAL TEXTS:
Editors' Foreword

The volumes in this series have been planned for those who are convinced that the Bible has a meaning for our life today, and who wish to enhance their skills as interpreters of the biblical texts. Such interpreters must necessarily engage themselves in two closely related tasks: (1) determining as much as possible the original meaning of the various biblical writings, and (2) determining in what respect these texts are still meaningful today. The objective of the present series is to keep both these tasks carefully in view and to provide assistance in relating the one to the other.

Because of this overall objective it would be wrong to regard the individual volumes in this series as commentaries, as homiletical expositions of selected texts, or as abstract discussions of "the hermeneutical problem." Rather, they have been written in order to identify and illustrate what is involved in relating the meaning of the biblical texts in their own times and places to their meaning in ours. Biblical commentaries and other technical reference works sometimes focus exclusively on the first, paying little or no attention to the second. On the other hand, many attempts to expound the contemporary "relevance" of biblical themes or passages pay scant attention to the intentions of the texts themselves. And although one of the standard topics of "hermeneutics" is how a text's original meaning relates to its present meaning, such discussions often employ highly technical philosophical language and proceed with little reference to concrete examples. By way of contrast, the present volumes are written in language that will be understood by scholars, clergy, and lay people alike, and they deal with concrete texts, actual problems of interpretation, and practical procedures for moving from "then" to "now."

Each contributor to this series is committed to three basic tasks: (1) a description of the salient features of the particular type of biblical literature or section of the canon assigned; (2) the identification and explanation of the basic assumptions which guide the contributor's analysis and explication of those materials; and (3) the discussion of possible contemporary meanings of representative texts, in view of the specified assumptions with which the interpreter approaches them. Considerations which should be borne in mind by the interpreter in reflecting upon contemporary meanings of these texts are introduced by the sign ● and are accentuated with a different style of type.

The assumptions brought to biblical interpretation may vary from one author to the next, and will undoubtedly vary from those of many readers. Nonetheless, we believe that the present series, by illustrating how careful interpreters carry out their tasks, will encourage readers to be more reflective about the way they interpret the Bible.

Lloyd R. Bailey, Sr.
Duke Divinity School

Victor P. Furnish
Perkins School of Theology
Southern Methodist University

CONTENTS

PREFACE

This book, we hope, will assist interpreters of the Pauline letters to do their work. We have not presumed to make specific "applications" of these texts, preferring instead to leave that to our readers. Nor have we codified the rules of the exegetical game or programmed the steps to sound interpretation, for both frequently promise more than they can deliver. Nor have we constructed a theoretical apparatus called "hermeneutics," which, when properly used, promises to thresh any text fed into it, unfailingly separating wheat from chaff. Instead, we have sought to place the interpreter among the interpreters, on the assumption that our readers will be helped most by learning from the interpreters who produced "the Pauline letters." At the same time, we have occasionally formulated observations and comments which might provoke further reflection and point the way to the meaning of those texts for our day.

A book such as this might have been organized in several ways; this way has a certain logic and seemed manageable to us. We have shared the responsibility for chapters 1, 2, and 3; the second subsection in each of these was written by

Mr. Furnish, the other subsections by Mr. Keck. Chapter 4 was the sole responsibility of Mr. Keck, and chapter 5 was the sole responsibility of Mr. Furnish. While we found it more difficult than we had anticipated to choose a limited number of representative passages for special attention, we believe our choices are defensible. And we hope that our comments about the interpretation of those passages will prove useful.

LEK
VPF

I. APPROACHING PAUL
AND HIS LETTERS

Among all the books of the New Testament, only at the Pauline letters is there a sign posted warning the reader to be careful:

> Our beloved brother Paul wrote to you according to the wisdom given him, speaking of this as he does in all his letters. There are some things in them hard to understand, which the ignorant and unstable twist to their own destruction, as they do the other scriptures. You therefore . . . knowing this beforehand, beware.

So writes the author of Second Peter (3:15-17) at the end of the New Testament era. Difficulties in interpreting Paul's letters arose even before this warning. Paul himself found it necessary to correct the understanding of his first letter (long lost) to the church in Corinth (1 Cor 5:9-13). Indeed, to a considerable degree the history of the interpretation of Paul is a history of conflict. Also today's interpreter of the Pauline letters faces no easy task, partly because one does not approach Paul in a vacuum. There are several "Pauls": the public Paul, the scholar's Paul, the church's Paul. By noting these at the outset, the interpreter can locate herself or himself on the map.

The Public Paul

Paul is one of those persons who regularly evokes strong opinions. He always has had his ardent defenders as well as his vigorous detractors, and both have been found among Christians and non-Christians. The history of Pauline interpretation shows that one can interpret him in either a sympathetic or a hostile way, and that interpreters in the one mode are likely to regard those in the other as misinterpreting the Apostle, as being blind to the obvious.

In many circles, Paul does not enjoy a good press; in fact, he is probably the most vilified Christian since Pentecost. It is not uncommon for Paul to bear the brunt of animus against Christianity itself—on the assumption that it is he who ruined what Jesus began. For example, in the nineteenth century the famous German anti-Semitic specialist in Semitic languages, Paul de Lagarde, expressed himself as follows:

> Everything that Paul says about Jesus and the gospel has no claim at all to reliability. . . . How can we still trust a church that is built on such a foundation? . . . Paul brought the Old Testament to us in the church, under whose influence the gospel has been ruined as much as possible. Paul blessed us with the Pharisaic exegesis which proves everything out of anything. . . . Paul carried home for us the Jewish sacrificial theory and everything connected with it: the entire . . . Jewish view of history has been loaded onto our backs by him. He did this under the vigorous opposition of the early

church which, as Jewish as it was, thought in a less Jewish way
than Paul.[1]

De Lagarde's virtual equation of Paul and Christianity is a
theme that runs through both anti-Pauline polemic and
pro-Pauline apologetics. Thus J. Gresham Machen, vigorous defender of orthodoxy in the first half of this century, not
only accounted for second-century Christianity's divergence
from Paul by claiming that "the Pauline doctrine of grace was
too wonderful and too divine to be understood fully by the
human mind and heart," but challenged scholars: "Explain
the origin of the religion of Paul and you have solved the
problem of the origin of Christianity."[2]

Today's antipathy to Paul is focused less on matters of
doctrine in the strict sense than on matters of ethics. Among
black theologians Paul is generally neglected, if not
disdained, because he is believed to have interpreted
Christianity as a religion of redemption of the soul, to have
fostered an accommodation with the slave-holding estab-
lishment and deferred salvation to the future coming of the
Lord. Moses, who led his people out of bondage, is regarded
more favorably than Paul, who left them there. For José
Miranda, on the other hand, this understanding (indebted to
the prevailing individualist reading of Paul) is a gross
distortion because "the efficacy of faith in making man
really and effectively just (that is, not an oppressor . . .) is
. . . of definitive importance for Paul." Paul's concern "is
with societies, civilizations, and cultures, and not with

[1]"Über das Verhältnis des deutschen Staates zu Theologie, Kirche, und
Religion; ein Versuch, Nicht-Theologen zu orientieren," quoted from A.
Hilgenfeld, review of D. F. Strauss, *Der alte und der neue Glaube, ZWTh* 16
(1873): 346-47.
[2]J. Gresham Machen, *The Origin of Paul's Religion* (Grand Rapids:
Eerdmans, 1947; original ed., 1925), pp. 6-7, 4-5.

individuals. . . . Paul's problem is mankind, the whole of
human civilization; it is to this that he wants to bring
salvation and justice."[3] Consequently Miranda sees Paul,
especially in the letter to the Romans, as an ally in the
struggle for social justice—but only if the interpretation of
Paul is freed from the received tradition.

Many have long regarded Paul as the architect of the
church's repression of women. Although the admonition
that wives be subject to their husbands is found not only in
Paul (see 1 Peter 3:1-6), the point is made repeatedly in the
letters accepted by the church as Pauline (Eph 5:21-33; Col
3:18; 1 Tim 2:9-15; Titus 2:5). Coupled with the explicit
command that women be silent in church (1 Cor 14:33b-40),
these counsels have indeed played a major role in "keeping
women in their place." Even if the paragraph from First
Corinthians is now widely regarded as an addition to the text,
and the others are not regarded as genuinely from Paul
himself but from Paulinists, it is as Pauline teaching that they
have exerted their influence. Consequently, a more careful
reading of what Paul himself said, and of what seems to have
been the practice in his churches, is underway. Indeed, it is
becoming apparent that women played important roles in his
churches. Thus the public image of Paul as a misogynist is
undergoing a major revision.

The widespread antipathies toward Paul will not be
dissipated easily, because he is also disdained for his
intolerance of opposition, for his capacity to be, on one page,
tender and affirming, and on another harsh and denuncia-
tory. He was a complex man in any case, not easy for
everyone to get along with. Had he been everybody's
favorite apostle, of course, he would not have written what

[3]José Miranda, *Marx and the Bible* (Maryknoll: Orbis Books, 1974),
pp. 174, 176.

he did, nor would he have become the dominant voice in the New Testament. In any case, Miranda is right in saying "there are many ways to consider Paul as a charlatan; the most exact way is the implicit: to overlook him."[4]

This book is an invitation to interpret him instead, and to do so by first taking account of the scholar's Paul.

The Scholar's Paul

The goal of what one may characterize generally as a "scholarly" approach to Paul and his letters is to describe and to explain as accurately and as impartially as possible just who Paul was, what he stood for, and what he achieved. The scholar attempts to portray Paul as a man of his own time and place, and to identify those people, events, and social forces that shaped his life, influenced his thought, and prompted him to act as he did. The scholar's interest in reconstructing "the historical Paul" is rooted, like much else in the Western world, in that concern for the critical investigation of nature and history which blossomed in the so-called Age of Enlightenment in seventeenth- and eighteenth-century Europe. Historical-critical methods of research were greatly refined and became widely accepted during the course of the nineteenth century and are, by and large, presupposed by twentieth-century scholars. Several of the fundamental concerns of historical scholarship may be illustrated, with reference specifically to the study of Paul.

Identification and Evaluation of the Sources. A historian's first task is always to identify the sources most pertinent to the subject under investigation and to develop appropriate methods for using them. In the case of Paul, the earliest sources are all to be found in the New Testament, but they are, nevertheless, of three different types.

[4]Miranda, *Marx and the Bible,* p. 164.

The scholar's most important source consists of those writings attributable to the Apostle himself. Thirteen letters, addressed to various churches and individuals, purport to be from Paul. At various times in the history of the church, the so-called Epistle to the Hebrews has also been counted among the Pauline letters, but it does not in itself make that claim, and its style and content prove that it is the work of some other distinguished Christian writer. There is general agreement that at least seven of the remaining thirteen letters were written by Paul himself, though they evidently have been subjected to a certain amount of subsequent editing and alteration. These seven unquestionably authentic Pauline letters are, in their canonical order: Romans, First Corinthians, Second Corinthians, Galatians, Philippians, First Thessalonians, and Philemon. Scholars differ in their conclusions about the authenticity of the remaining six, some or all of which, though bearing Paul's name, may have been written by others after the Apostle's death.

The six letters whose authenticity is disputed are, in their canonical order: Ephesians, Colossians, Second Thessalonians, and the Pastoral Epistles (1 Tim, 2 Tim, and Titus). These constitute a second and distinct group of sources from which the Paul of modern scholarship derives. The Pastoral Epistles are the ones most widely regarded as Pseudo- or Deutero-Pauline, and Ephesians, too, is very commonly assigned to a later writer. Scholarly opinion is more divided about the authorship of Colossians, and while some question the authenticity of Second Thessalonians, probably the majority of interpreters regard it as the Apostle's own. The fact remains, however, that the origin of six of the thirteen Pauline letters in the New Testament is disputed to one degree or another, and that most scholarly interpretations of Paul take this into account. Thus (to cite only a few examples), the scholar's Paul does not speak of Christ as the

"head of the body," for that metaphor is found only in
Ephesians and Colossians; the scholar's Paul issues no
admonitions to wives, children, and slaves to be subject,
respectively, to their husbands, parents, and masters, for
these are found, again, only in Ephesians and Colossians; the
scholar's Paul provides no information about "the lawless
one" who will precede the Lord's return at the close of
history, for this is found only in Second Thessalonians; and
the scholar's Paul offers no lists of qualifications for bishops
and other church officials, since these are found only in the
Pastoral Epistles. These disputed letters, however edifying,
are classified among the *secondary* sources. While they may
in certain respects supplement or enhance the understanding
of Paul to be gained from the unquestionably authentic
letters, it is the latter from which the historian's *primary* data
regarding Paul's life and thought are derived.

The scholar's third major source for the study of Paul is the
canonical Acts of the Apostles which, despite its traditional
title, focuses especially on Paul, whom it seems not to
include among the apostles. It is clear that the Gospel of
Luke and the book of Acts constitute one two-volume work
composed by a single author. If, as the tradition says and as
certain modern interpreters still believe, that author was
indeed Luke, whom Paul referred to as one of his "fellow
workers" (Phlm 24) and who is described as "the beloved
physician" (Col 4:14), then Acts would have special value as
the account of one who himself participated in some of the
events reported. There are, however, so many important
discrepancies between what one learns of Paul from his own
letters and the way he is presented in Acts that the Lucan
authorship of Acts cannot be affirmed with any confidence.
While the author has undoubtedly relied upon certain
traditions about Paul which are historically valuable, these
have been conformed to the author's own purposes, one of

which was to portray the apostolic age as a time when, unified and empowered by the Holy Spirit, believers were enabled to bear witness to the gospel throughout the world (see, e.g., Acts 1:8; 23:11). Thus Acts minimizes the sort of tension between Paul and Peter one reads about in Galatians 2:11-14 and is silent about the opposition Paul met from other Christians in places like Corinth. Moreover, while the letters show that the saving power of the cross (1 Cor, chaps 1, 2), justification by faith (Rom, Gal), and the distinctiveness of his own apostolic calling (2 Cor) were major themes of Paul's preaching and teaching, the "Pauline speeches" of Acts emphasize the resurrection, not the cross, and contain nothing about justification by faith or Paul's apostolic vocation. The scholar's Paul, therefore, is not derived primarily from the book of Acts. As a secondary source, Acts, like the six disputed letters, is used with the greatest caution only to confirm, clarify, and elaborate what is already known on the basis of the authentic letters alone. Most scholars are unwilling to accredit data from Acts which contradict evidence from the letters or which would involve any substantial alteration in the information these letters, taken by themselves, disclose about Paul's life and thought.

Analysis of the Sources. The process of identifying pertinent sources, of distinguishing between those of primary and those of secondary importance, and of developing appropriate methods for using them, at the same time involves ascertaining their nature and their function. In the case of Paul, this means giving close attention not only to the literary form, style, and function of his certainly authentic letters, but also to the form, style, and function of the disputed letters and of Acts. Since Acts is best discussed in connection with the Gospel of Luke,[5]

[5]See, e.g., F. B. Craddock, *The Gospels,* Interpreting Biblical Texts (Nashville: Abingdon Press, 1981), pp. 94-100.

and since some of the special features and functions of the disputed letters are characterized in chapter 5, we may restrict ourselves here to a few general comments about the nature and function of the seven undisputed letters.

First, it is important to remember that these were *letters to congregations,* not to individuals. The letter to Philemon is only a partial exception because, while it appealed to that one Christian brother specifically, it was addressed also to Apphia, Archippus, and an entire house-church (vv 1-2). Thus none of Paul's letters was a strictly private communication. They were all "semipublic," in that Paul clearly intended for them to be shared with all the members of the Christian communities in the places to which they were addressed. One may presume that, upon receiving a letter from Paul, the leaders of the local congregation would have read it aloud the next time believers were gathered for worship. Indeed, Paul's custom of opening and closing his letters with an apostolic blessing (e.g., Rom 1:7*b*; 15:33; 1 Thess 1:1*c*; 5:28; Phlm 3, 25) suggests that the Apostle may have taken the worship setting into account as he wrote. It must be emphasized, however, that these letters are not sermons. They are more like pastoral letters, written for the most part to congregations Paul himself had established (Rom and Phlm are the exceptions) and for which he felt some special responsibility.

Second, while each of the Pauline letters had its own specific occasion and purpose, all served the general and fundamental purpose of providing *an apostolic presence* even while the Apostle was physically absent. Paul was clearly aware of this function of his letters (see Rom 15:22-25; 1 Cor 1:23–2:4; Phil 1:27; 2:12), even when a particular letter was sent off only shortly before his own departure for the same place, as in the case of Second Corinthians, chapters 10 through 13 (see 13:10). One must recognize not only that the letters were meant to substitute, however inadequately, for his actual presence, but that they were written with a sense of apostolic authority. They were not dispatched as letters simply from a friend or acquaintance. They were intended to be read as communications from one who had been set apart to serve the gospel in a special way (see Rom 1:1-6; 1 Cor 1:1; Gal 1:1, etc.), one who, indeed, could claim to "have the Spirit of God" (1 Cor 7:40*b*).

Third, and closely related to the second point, scholarly analysis of Paul's letters has shown that they were all *situation-specific*. None was addressed "to the church at large," or even "to all the Pauline congregations." Although Galatians was addressed to several congregations ("To the churches of Galatia," Gal 1:2*b*), the matters taken up there are specifically "Galatian issues," as the whole letter makes clear (Gal 1:6-9; 3:1-5; 4:12-20, etc.). The same can be said about First Thessalonians (see esp. chap 4), First Corinthians (see esp. 7:1, "Now concerning the matters about which you wrote"), Second Corinthians (see esp. 1:15–2:11; 12:14–13:4), Philippians (e.g., 2:19-30; 4:2-3; 14:20), and Philemon (which deals exclusively with the case of Onesimus). The Letter to the Romans, sent to Christians in a city Paul had not yet visited, was in certain respects more generally conceived and written. However, this letter too was situation-specific, in that Paul's own situation had prompted him to write. On one hand, he needed support from the Roman Christians in order to launch a mission to Spain, and on the other, he was constrained—more immediately—to go to Jerusalem with a "contribution for the poor among the saints" (Rom 15:14-33; cf. 1:9-15). Thus scholarly studies of Romans, no less than scholarly studies of Paul's other letters, characteristically attempt to identify the specific situation which occasioned its writing and influenced its contents.

Fourth, despite the fact that our primary sources for Paul are letters called forth by specific situations and addressed to particular congregations, scholarly analysis has shown that they were *organized and composed with some care.* Like most of his contemporaries, the Apostle seems to have dictated his letters to a professional scribe (see Rom 16:22), sometimes affixing a closing paragraph in his own hand (1 Cor 16:21; Gal 6:11). Most of the Apostle's letters are longer than the ordinary hellenistic letter, however, and some or all of them may have been written over a period of several days. While they generally follow the conventional form of ancient letters, they do so with certain modifications appropriate to their special apostolic function: the opening salutations usually emphasize the writer's authoritative position and describe in some way the Christian calling of the addressee (Rom 1:1-7; 1 Cor 1:1-3, etc.; contrast the more typically hellenistic salutation of Jas 1:1); there usually follows an extended paragraph thanking (or blessing) God for the faith and conduct of the addressees (in 1 Thess this seems to extend from 1:2 clear through chap 3; only Gal lacks such a section); the letter bodies often include comments on a number of topics (the single appeal contained in Phlm is more typical of ancient letters), with carefully developed arguments and extensive exposition of Scripture or appeals to other traditional materials; and as noted above, opening and closing apostolic blessings are standard. While the Pauline letters are not polished essays, neither are they impromptu notes carelessly dashed off and oblivious to the requirements of form, style, and argument.

Reconstruction of the Social Setting Within Which the Sources Originated. Although the primary sources from which modern scholarship derives its understanding of Paul are exclusively canonical, the process of canonization took place within the Christian community, just as the individual letters had been prompted by various specific situations Paul confronted during the course of his ministry. Therefore another aspect of the scholarly investigation of Paul is the attempt to reconstruct, insofar as possible, the broader social setting within which the Apostle preached, established congregations, and exercised pastoral oversight. This involves an analysis of Paul's place within the Christian movement as a whole, including his relationships with his co-workers and with the leaders of the Jerusalem church, especially Peter. It also involves the effort to understand Paul within the still broader context of Greco-Roman society, including its political and economic institutions, its social customs, its intellectual and cultural attainments, and its religious life. This analysis enables us to see the Apostle as something more than a pasteboard figure cut out of the canon. It helps us experience him as a multidimensional figure, a person whose distinctive religious insights and contributions can be adequately assessed only when we understand how much he shared with and was influenced by the society in which he lived. For this task of understanding Paul's world, the scholar has available many additional primary sources—mainly non-Christian—including literary works, inscriptions, and various remains unearthed by archaeologists.

Synthesis of the Data. Once the data from all available sources have been gathered, sorted, and critically evaluated, the scholar sets about synthesizing them into a coherent, historically credible description of Paul, his gospel, and his ministry. The Paul that emerges from this whole process is, admittedly, a hypothetical construct and, in that sense, a "synthetic Paul." But this is true in principle of any attempt to recover and reconstruct the past, whether one's subject be

Plato or Charlemagne or Abraham Lincoln. There is, of course, no *one* "scholar's Paul," for the same data can be interpreted and synthesized differently—just as Paul's words and actions were perceived and interpreted differently by his contemporaries. Despite this, there is certainly enough substantial scholarly agreement on the major features of Paul's life and ministry to facilitate constructive debate about the various points on which consensus is more difficult to achieve.

This may be illustrated by referring to the matter of Pauline chronology. The scholar would like to be able to study Paul's letters in the order in which they were written and to relate their contents, insofar as possible, to Paul's experiences and to known events, both within the Christian movement and in society at large. There is, in fact, general agreement about an overall chronological framework, and even about a few rough dates:

Activity as persecutor of the church (early 30s).

Conversion (mid-30s).

First visit to Jerusalem (late 30s).

Missionary activities in Asia Minor and Greece (late 40s and early 50s), with letters to Thessalonica (1 Thess) and Corinth (see 1 Cor 5:9), and a second visit to Jerusalem.

Extended residence in Ephesus (mid-50s) and further correspondence with the Corinthians (at least 1 Cor).

Further visits to congregations in Macedonia and Greece (mid- to late 50s), further correspondence with Corinth (2 Cor), and a letter to Rome.

Last visit to Jerusalem (late 50s), arrest, imprisonment in Caesarea.

Voyage to Rome (late 50s), eventual execution there (early 60s).

There are, however, many specific questions relating to this general outline on which scholars cordially disagree:

What exactly was Paul doing between the time of his conversion and the period of his intense activity in Asia Minor and Greece?

Did Paul's long stay in Ephesus include a period of imprisonment, and were Philippians and Philemon, both written in prison, sent from there or—later—from Caesarea or from Rome?

When and where was Galatians written?

Are any of the canonical letters composites of originally separate communications (Rom? 1 Cor? 2 Cor? Phil?), and if so, in what order and under what circumstances were the originally separate letters dispatched?

To scholars, these and many similar questions are by no means unimportant, for a fundamental concern of Pauline scholarship is to understand the Apostle's life and ministry in essentially historical terms and to interpret his letters, and therefore his thought, in the light of his life experiences and relationships. Complex though the scholar's Paul may be, this Paul can enrich and enlarge the church's Paul.

The Church's Paul

The church's Paul is the Paul of the New Testament canon—the man whom thirteen letters name as author, plus the Paul who dominates the book of Acts from chapter 13 onward. The church's Paul is also known as Saint Paul—a phrase he would have repudiated because it singles him out as a super-Christian; for Paul, all Christians were "saints," or "holy ones," because that was a term for God's people. In the church, Paul is also known as the Apostle, another phrase he would have rejected—though he insisted he was a bonafide apostle. In the church Paul also enjoys the reputation of being *the* great missionary—a reputation he doubtless would have enjoyed (see 1 Cor 15:10). There are, to be sure, additional interesting nuances. For example, it has sometimes been said that Eastern Orthodoxy is Johannine, Roman Catholicism is Petrine, and Protestantism is Pauline—a suggestive distortion. Interestingly enough, despite the flood tide of pastoral care in today's church, scarcely anyone thinks of Paul as a pastor—though he evidently took this aspect of his work quite seriously (see, e.g., 1 Thess 3:9-12).

More important, the Paul whom the church presents to its congregations is a deliberately restricted Paul. Unless people participate in church school classes or other educational programs that study Scripture seriously, the Bible they hear is virtually limited to those parts they hear in church. People who attend churches that use a set order of readings (a lectionary) are almost certain to hear a wider range of Scripture than do those who attend churches in which the minister reads whatever seems appropriate. Yet the typical lectionary abbreviates Paul. To be sure, even on a three-year cycle of readings, much of the Bible must be omitted, and some of it probably should be, including some of the Pauline letters (e.g., most of Rom 16 is a list of greetings; 2 Cor 7 deals with the intricacies of Paul's relations with the Corinthians). Still, when due allowance has been made for the limits of time and for the relative unsuitability of certain passages, the fact remains: Even the person who never "missed a Sunday" has heard but part of Paul. Indeed, almost as much of the thirteen canonical letters is omitted as is read.

The data provided by the *Lutheran Book of Worship* and the proposed ecumenical lectionary reveal an effort to provide a series of readings from the same epistle (esp. Rom,

1 Cor, Eph); at the same time, there is a good deal of "bouncing around," so that it may be weeks—and sometimes years—before the next passage is read (e.g., Gal 4:4-7 is read during the first year; the second year omits Gal entirely; Gal 5 appears in the third year, while Gal 4:8-31 is never read). Philemon is read in part every third year, Titus "never on Sunday" (Titus is read on Christmas Day).

The omissions include some rather important passages:

Rom	1:8–3:20	an indictment of all humanity, the background for Paul's exposition of justification by faith
	6:17-21	Paul's interpretation of baptism for ethics
	9:6-33	God's sovereign freedom in election
	11:16-28	Paul's allegory of the olive tree (Gentiles are "grafted into" Israel.)
	12:9-21	exhortations ending with "Do not be overcome by evil, but overcome evil with good."
1 Cor	7:1-28, 32-40	Paul's counsel on marriage and divorce
	12:1-21	Paul's exposition of one Spirit, many gifts
	14:1-11, 21-40	most of the discussion of "tonguespeaking"

2 Cor 9:1–12:6, 11-21	Paul's most eloquent interpretation of his apostleship
1 Thess 5:12-15	ethical exhortations
Eph 6:1-9	table of duties to one another in the household
Col 3:18-25	table of duties to one another in the household
2 Thess 2:1-12	the apocalyptic heart of that letter
1 Tim 2:9–5:25	admonitions concerning women, bishops, deacons, "heretics," widows, etc.

Moreover, insofar as the sermons might not deal with the epistle passage that *is* read, a good deal of Paul (and Deutero-Paul) will almost certainly never be interpreted either. Interestingly, the lectionary used by Lutherans contains readings from only that part of Acts which deals with Paul—three selections from Acts 13–14 (Paul's preaching). The narratives of Paul's work are completely in eclipse.

What does this tell the interpreter? One learns that one must compensate for the neglected Paul and Deutero-Paul if one is to make Pauline and Paulinist theology intelligible as a coherent understanding of the Christian faith; that mere allusions to the work of Paul (as reported in Acts 13–28) are wasted on all hearers who have not become acquainted with these stories in other contexts; that Paul's pastoral concerns will scarcely surface in the context of the Sunday morning reading of Scripture. And that the interpreter of the Pauline letters has a clear opportunity.

II. THE INTERPRETER'S CHOICES

The literate interpreter of the Pauline letters soon discovers a number of forks in the road—points at which decisions become unavoidable, not simply because the texts themselves can be read in more than one way. For example, the interpreter will choose whether to interpret Paul's thought primarily in light of his Jewish heritage or against the background of the religiosity of the Greco-Roman world. The second part of this chapter outlines some of those choices.

The interpreter faces choices also about her or his own work, and it is with these that the first part of this chapter is concerned. Probably the most far-reaching decision concerns the type of interpretation that will be undertaken. It is somewhat ironic that just when the historical-critical method has won almost universal acceptance as a method that enables students from a wide spectrum of theological persuasions to converse fruitfully, there should emerge modes of interpretation which emphasize other forms of inquiry. Because this book discusses the interpretation of the Pauline letters on the basis of the still prevalent historical-critical method, a word about other modes is appropriate.

Though by no means unified, these other modes have in common a concern for the text as a text, an understanding of how the text "works." In the case of narrative texts (e.g., the Gospels or Acts), the focus is not on the events narrated but on the narration itself—matters of plot, story line, character portrayal, and the like. In the case of discursive texts (e.g., treatises like Heb or the letters), the focus is on the interplay of the parts in the articulation of thought, with considerable attention to the distinction between what is put into words "on the surface" and the "deep structure"—the configuration of convictions, or "semantic universe," which actually governs what *is* put into words and what *can* be put into words. This semantic universe determines what can be formulated, just as a language determines what can be said and how one can say it. Some have pressed this line of reasoning to the point that the ultimate goal is to expose the structure and working of the human mind itself. Others are content to work nearer the "surface," to explore how characters are paired in narratives or to probe antinomies of ideas. In obtaining perspective, one compares texts and elements of texts in order to discern common traits and shared configurations in similar types of material. In other words, this literary approach (overlapping with "structuralist" approaches) is concerned with *generic* relationships, whereas the historical-critical approach seeks *genetic* relationships—antecedents and influences which account for a phenomenon in a given text. The generic inquiry compares the Synoptic Gospels, for example, in order to discern their common qualities and proceeds to account for them by relating those texts to similar narratives, from whatever culture or date. In other words, this literary-linguistic approach works *synchronically,* whereas the discerning of influences, causes and effects, revisions, and the like, which characterizes historical inquiry, works *diachronically*—across *chronos,* time.

These two modes of inquiry and interpretation can be complementary, and in the future probably will be. In any case, each has its own rationale, its own integrity, its own possibilities and limits (e.g., there is a "generic fallacy" as well as a "genetic fallacy"). Each was undertaken in order to deal with a certain range of questions. In the discussion that follows, it is the historical-critical mode that will be in focus, because the writers are persuaded that it is this approach that has generated the questions on the minds of most interpreters of the Pauline letters.

Distinguishing Modes of Work

Historical-critical inquiry came to dominate biblical study in order to distinguish the real past from the perceived and received past. For a variety of reasons, it was deemed necessary to reconstruct the past "as it really was." This effort was directed not only toward events in order to distinguish "fact" from report, but also toward the history of ideas and institutions in order to read every text in light of its (reconstructed) original setting. Like events, ideas were accounted for in light of antecedents and influences. Where they could not be verified, they were inferred. This is why a historical-critical method majors in genetic relationships. Nourished by archaeological finds ranging from papyri in Egypt to inscriptions in the Aegean basin, to the Dead Sea Scrolls in the Holy Land, scholarship placed every biblical text, word, idea, and practice in the cultural setting of antiquity; moreover, the enterprise has been an astounding success, for repeatedly, the biblical text has been understood more accurately than before.

In the course of the past two centuries the historical-critical enterprise has become enormously sophisticated, having developed a whole battery of procedures for locating every aspect of the text in its proper historical context—*text* criticism (establishing the wording of the text), *source* criticism (determining whether earlier texts were used), *form* criticism (ascertaining the correlation between the form of the material and its function, especially for material transmitted orally), and *redaction* criticism (noting how the writer used the materials received).[1] Those who study the Pauline letters in the historical-critical mode accumulate a vast amount of information about these letters and their contexts. Questions arise, too: Does one gain understanding? Does one become a more competent interpreter? And some would add: Does learning to "explain the Bible" lead one to "explain it away"?

With regard to these questions, one should be suspicious of answers easily given and swiftly reached. Moreover, there are important differences between *explanation, understanding,* and *interpretation,* even though they also overlap. If these differences are identified, the interpreter can choose their relative importance in a given situation.

1. *Explanation* refers to the attempt to account for the text in terms of historical causes. As vital as explanation may be for understanding and interpretation, it is not to be confused with them. Nor should it be overlooked that the texts themselves call for explanation, and at many levels. In the study of texts—biblical texts included—one axiom is to be followed: Take nothing for granted; its corollary: There is a reason for everything (whether or not one is able to discover it). The sheer existence of the text calls for

[1]Examples are provided below: text criticism, p. 60; source criticism, pp. 126-40; form criticism, pp. 117-19; redaction criticism, pp. 78-81.

explanation: Why was it written? and What did the writer expect it to accomplish? These two questions, though intimately related, are not identical. The letter to Philemon was written because Onesimus, Philemon's slave, had fled to Paul, who sent him back with the letter. But what was the letter to accomplish, besides intervention on behalf of the runaway? It is often proposed that the real aim of the letter was to gain Onesimus' freedom so that he could rejoin Paul's circle.

Explanation has to do not only with the wording of the text (text criticism, or lower criticism, as it used to be called) but also with its content (higher criticism, as it was known). Why does Paul say what he says, and why does he say it in exactly this way and not in some other way? Virtually every aspect of the text and the phenomena in it are susceptible to explanations which account for what lies before the reader. The Pauline letters vary greatly in the degree to which they yield explanatory answers to these rudimentary questions; moreover, every accounting for the content of these letters entails consequences for the way one pictures the emergence of early Christianity as a whole.

In general, it is easier to account for the content of the genuine letters than for that of the Deutero-Pauline letters. The reason is clear: In dealing with the uncontested letters we have an identifiable author at a generally specifiable time and place. In the case of the Deutero-Pauline letters one must account for the content, while at the same time positing unidentifiable authors writing at times and places no longer recoverable. When Second Thessalonians (2:2) warns the reader "not to be quickly shaken in mind or excited, either by spirit or by word, or by a letter purporting to be from us, to the effect that the day of the Lord has come," it is clear enough that what follows is an attempt to counteract a letter already in circulation. So now the explanatory process involves accounting for both the letter we have and the one denounced.

That the explanatory process entails reconstructing the course of early Christianity is clear from the fact that, just as Paul's own letters lead us back into the early years of the church, so those written in his name lead us forward into the second, if not the third generation. Paul's letters are the oldest texts in the New Testament, First Thessalonians antedating the oldest Gospel, Mark, by almost two decades. Moreover, as will be noted in chapter 4, embedded in Paul's letters are fixed traditions that go back to the years shortly after the lifetime of Jesus. Thus one can reconstruct "Pauline Christianity" from its earliest pre-Pauline days (the Christianity into which Paul was baptized) to its lineaments several generations later, although the gaps in information are enormous. In other words, to "explain" Paul historically is to account for what he says by attending to his interaction with his contemporary readers, and also to his antecedents on the one hand and to his legacy on the other. The historian sees that alongside this Pauline stream ran other currents, not apparently influenced by Paul or influencing him—the Johannine, the Synoptic, and the Jacobean (a form of Jewish Christianity which looked to James, the Lord's brother). It is not surprising that the explanatory process should appeal to those who enjoy reading detective stories, just as it should repel those who wish to understand Paul directly for the sake of their spiritual and moral well-being.

It is important to know what to expect from explanation. First, the game of historical explanation must be played consistently and without hesitation, or it cannot be played convincingly at all. Second, historical questions require historical answers—that is, answers based on public evidence publicly assessed by those competent to do so.

Historical explanation excludes all appeal to what the Holy Spirit, for example, has revealed to the student. Who wrote the Pastoral Epistles? This is a historical question; even if for some the answer has religious significance, the answer itself cannot be determined by that significance. Third, explanations are not evidence but are causal relationships posited on the basis of probabilities for which warrants can be adduced. The persuasiveness of the warrants and the probabilities varies from student to student, so it is not surprising that many points remain unsettled. In general, what marks some explanations as "conservative" is not simply the character of the student's theology, but also the tendency to put the burden of proof on the one who challenges the tradition; whereas "radical" critics require the tradition to maintain itself in the face of a "hermeneutics of suspicion." Fourth, to explain a text historically is not to "explain it away," but to bring it into reality. What the explanatory process dissipates is often no more than a mystique grounded in misconception. Above all, explanation does not annul the biblical text as the vehicle for God's Word. The claim that God "speaks" through the biblical text is totally beyond the bounds of historical inquiry. The historian can deal with the belief about God's Word and the consequences of that belief—that can be explained. God's Word, however, can only be confessed.

2. If explanation is relatively straightforward and public, *understanding* is subtle and personal. Whereas the explanatory process requires knowledge to assess evidence and historical thinking to discern causal relationships and weigh warrants, understanding requires both the capacity to grasp coherences and the ability to think with the text about the subject matter.

To understand a text, a person, a movement, a community, or an era historically is to see the parts in relationship to one another in an intelligible whole. Manifestly, a sharp line cannot be drawn between explanation and understanding, because each impinges on the other. As implied above, explaining Pauline Christianity entails understanding it as a discernible type and seeing it in relation to other types. When one concentrates on a particular text—say First Thessalonians—understanding it requires seeing it also in relation to the whole Pauline corpus. Did the apocalyptic teaching (1 Thess 4:13–5:11) remain a constant element in Paul's thought? Or was it his particular response to a one-time local problem? Or was it a set of ideas which he later modified or abandoned? (There is no explicit reference to the coming of Christ in Romans.) Likewise, one will compare the apocalyptic teaching in First Thessalonians with that in Second Thessalonians, and also with apocalyptic passages elsewhere in the New Testament, in order to locate this particular teaching in the overall picture of apocalyptic in early Christianity.

Above all, understanding entails thinking with the text and its author about the subject matter. To do so, one must position oneself with the writer, assume (at least for the moment) the writer's standpoint and way of thinking. For example, in Romans 9–11 Paul addresses head on the problems posed by the Jews' rejection of the gospel, which, according to Paul's convictions, they should have accepted as the fulfillment of God's ways with the chosen people. These chapters bristle with matters to be explained, accounted for: the choice of Old Testament texts, the wording of the quotations, the exegetical methods Paul uses, and so on. But one does not really understand these chapters until one stands with Paul and feels with him the weight of the problem; until one grasps the inner coherence between what is said here and what is developed earlier in the letter; until one's thinking-with-Paul takes account of the way Mark, Matthew, and John wrestle with the same issue.

Understanding is not agreement; in fact, it may be more difficult to understand what one agrees with than that from which one differs, precisely because understanding entails a grasp of the whole, a "gestaltic" perception of the parts in relation to one another—something hard to grasp regarding one's own ideas or "semantic universe." To understand what differs summons one to set aside prejudicial attitudes and to suspend antipathies in order to attend carefully and openly to what is at hand. For instance, as long as one approaches the Pastorals with a typical Protestant prejudice against their flattened view that faith is confidence in reliable teaching, one will scarcely lay hold of their author's mentality. This suspension of antipathies (and enthusiasms!) is not a matter of creating a feigned "objectivity," a pretended disinterest for the sake of truth. It is simply a (actually not simple) matter of taking responsibility for one's readiness to learn from the text. It is a willingness to bring one's concern for the subject matter into the open where it can be addressed by the text, and perhaps be illumined, corrected, or even rejected by the text. To seek understanding is to risk.

There are neither rules for understanding nor procedures for attaining it, for there is something intuitive, or "divinatory," about it. Because understanding is intimately linked to insight, it may accrue gradually, or it may occur suddenly in a moment of illumination—though often such moments have been preceded by patient study and brooding over the subject matter. This is why understanding is intensely personal, for each reader brings a different life experience (as well as knowledge) to the text. There may be a more or less correct explanation of phenomena in the text (wording, use of tradition, formative factors in its creation, etc.), but there is no such thing as "the correct" understanding of its subject matter. Understandings can be compared critically and assessed, of course. Indeed, one assesses one's own understanding, especially in retrospect, because further reflection and study often disclose that an earlier understanding—even one which seemed so clear and self-evident—was in fact at least a partial misunderstanding or a superficial grasp of the matter.

Given this personal quality, it is not surprising that understanding presupposes a capacity to comprehend the subject matter. Persons who lack the ability to think abstractly cannot understand treatises on logic. Fortunately, capacities, including the capacity to think theologically, can be developed, and logical thinking is what many passages in the Pauline corpus require. In turn, acquiring an understanding of these letters enlarges one's capacity as a theologian or as a historian. One learns not only what Paul and his successors thought about, but how they thought. Indeed, one who has begun to learn by the case method should find it possible to learn theology by approaching the Pauline letters as a series of "cases."

3. Understanding is essential to *interpretation*—the process of restating what is understood. Interpretation occurs at many levels, including translation itself. As a matter of fact, interpretation is the translation of the subject matter into another idiom in order to make it more accessible. Interpretation has to do with the transition from understanding "what it meant" to saying "what it means." The need for interpretation arises whenever there is a gap between the "semantic world" of the text in its original setting and that in which it is being read. Then words, phrases, ideas, and motifs in the text are available only dimly, if at all, to the reader in a different setting. As more historical work reconstructs the environment in which a text

came into existence, in order to understand it in its "natural habitat," the greater the need to interpret, to translate not only words but ideas.

Paraphrase is a common form of such interpretive effort. It takes a variety of forms, ranging from the restatement of the idea in the New English Bible to Clarence Jordan's *Cotton Patch Version,* which has Paul writing letters to Christians in the Sunbelt cities and to this nation's "Rome," Washington, D.C. Jordan's intent is clear—to find words, ideas, and social realities in modern southern experience which allow him to express Paul's point in such a way that its impact will approximate Jordan's understanding of the original Greek. The folksy anachronism intends to enable modern southern white Christians to hear Paul in their own idiom.

It is useful to reflect on the difference between explanation and interpretation and to see how understanding mediates between them, because it is requisite for both. In explanation, one helps the reader enter a different world by identifying items in it and/or by accounting for their being there. The explainer is a tour guide who takes the modern reader into antiquity and tries to make it intelligible. The greater the difference between the world of the beholder and that of the beheld, the more the beholder is aware that he or she does not live there. A great deal of Bible study is essentially explanation. The interpreter, on the other hand, moves in the opposite direction—bringing the distant and ancient world forward into that of the reader. In language that does not need to be explained but can make its point directly, the interpreter attempts to state his or her understanding of the subject matter expressed in the text.

Clearly, if one looks for exact equivalence, interpretation always includes a degree of distortion because the idea is being carried across the gap between two worlds. One risks distortion in order to make one's understanding of the text available, to mediate its perceived significance, to release its meaning into a different world where it can assert itself. Because exact equivalence is not a possibility, interpretations are to be assessed in terms of aptness in relation to the text and appropriateness in relation to the reader. Nor should one expect that the total meaning of a word or idea can be restated in another idiom or that the new articulation will not add meaning and connotations of its own. Interpretation risks both loss and gain.

Because historical explanation and understanding are foundational for interpretation, the rest of this book concentrates on explanation in order to foster understanding and interpretation. In the effort to explain and understand Paul, one must make some basic choices.

Choosing Meaningful Contexts

Each specific Pauline text must be explained and understood, not only with reference to its immediate literary context, which extends to the entire letter of which it is a part, but also with reference to the Apostle's life, thought, and ministry as a whole. The necessity of this is clear enough when a text is dealing with concrete matters—for example, Paul's collection for the Jerusalem church. Each of the several texts which refer to that project (Rom 15:14-33; 1 Cor 16:1-4; 2 Cor 8–9; Gal 2:1-10) must first be studied in its own specific context. But taken together, these texts begin to disclose a broader context, and as that broader context emerges, one's understanding of the specific texts (and contexts) is substantially enhanced. The same is true when a particular text deals with ideas or concepts such as the role of the Law. For example, while the discussion of the Law in Romans 7:7-25 must be interpreted initially within Romans as a whole (taking account of such passages as 2:12–4:25 and

9:30–10:13), it must also be read within the still wider context
of Paul's own Pharisaic background (see Gal 1:13-14; Phil
3:4-5), his call to apostleship (Gal 1:15-16; Phil 3:7-11), his
relationship with the Jerusalem apostles (Gal 2:1-10, 11-21),
and his understanding of the meaning of Jesus' crucifixion
(see esp. Gal 3–4).

It should be clear enough from these two examples that an
important part of the interpreter's task is to ascertain the
several contexts within which a given passage, theme, or
topic needs to be examined. Only in this way may one arrive
at an understanding that is consistent with and that also can
make a contribution to one's understanding of Paul's life and
ministry as a whole. The relating of a text to its various
contexts is therefore an extremely critical aspect of
interpretation, and one needs to be aware of the kinds of
choices this responsibility thrusts upon the interpreter.
One's view of what Paul himself did or did not write will
affect the way one delimits the larger literary context within
which a specific text is studied. One's judgment about the
Apostle's cultural heritage will often influence one's
understanding of specific words, metaphors, and concepts.
What one supposes about Paul's psychic life and religious
experience will have a bearing on one's estimate of his
motives and goals. And what one identifies as the theological
center of Paul's gospel will, in large part, determine the way
all other aspects of his preaching and teaching are construed.
Each of these points deserves some further comment.

Delimiting the Literary Context. In the vocabulary of
biblical exegesis, *pericope* (pě-rĭk´ō-pē, "cut around") refers
to a relatively short passage (perhaps only a paragraph or
two) in which, however, one complete thought or topic is
introduced, developed, and at least provisionally concluded.
A pericope, then, is a more or less self-contained unit within
a larger text. In delimiting the literary context of any given

sentence or statement, the interpreter's first responsibility is to identify the pericope within which it stands. This is sometimes quite easy (e.g., the salutations in Paul's letters are readily identifiable pericopes), but it is often rather difficult (e.g., is Paul's reference to his flight from Damascus [2 Cor 11:32-33] a self-contained unit, or is it part of a larger pericope which includes vv 30-31 [see RSV], or perhaps even vv 28-31 [see NEB]?). Pericopes, in turn, must be read within the broader context of the whole document and its various identifiable subsections. Finally, the document itself, when it is not the only one surviving from its author, needs to be set within the overall context of that writer's total literary production.

In the case of the Pauline letters, one must decide whether to restrict one's view of the larger literary context of individual pericopes to those letters whose authenticity is generally undisputed (see p. 16), or whether one or more of the disputed letters is to be included as part of that wider context. If, for example, one accepts the Pauline authorship of Colossians, the reference there to baptism as involving the believer's death *and* resurrection with Christ (Col 2:12) might well be decisive in causing one to interpret the more ambiguous statements of Romans 6:4, 5 in the same way. Or again, one who accepts the Pastoral Epistles as genuinely Pauline will be apt to interpret the "bishops and deacons" of Philippians 1:1 as holding well-defined offices, while one who regards the Pastorals as Deutero-Pauline is likely to understand the terms much more generally, or may even question whether they originally stood in the text. One's judgment about the authorship of the disputed letters and the firmness or tentativeness with which one holds to it are in a sense less important than the awareness that one's judgment in the matter will affect, sometimes decisively,

one's interpretation. Very often differences of interpretation encountered in the commentaries and other literature
on Paul can also be traced, at least in part, to disagreement
about the broader literary context within which individual
passages and letters should be read.

Understanding Paul's Cultural Heritage. One's judgment
about Paul's cultural heritage will also influence the way one
reads and interprets his letters. That Paul was born into a
Jewish family is beyond dispute, and we have his own
testimony that until his conversion to Christianity he had
been an earnest practitioner of the Jewish Law (Rom 11:1; 2
Cor 11:22; Gal 1:13-14; Phil 3:4-6; cf. Rom 9:1-3). While all
students of Paul can agree on this much, there is substantial
disagreement about the extent to which Paul, even before his
conversion and dedication to a Gentile mission, had been
acculturated to hellenistic society.

Some interpreters believe that the Apostle's description of
himself as "a Hebrew born of Hebrews" (Phil 3:5; cf. 2 Cor
11:22) is proof that he could read Hebrew, and perhaps even
that his first language was Aramaic, a closely related Semitic
tongue spoken by many Jews in his day. Then, accepting the
accuracy of the reference in Acts 22:3 to Paul's having
studied the Law under the renowned Gamaliel in Jerusalem,
and pointing out that the Apostle himself writes of having
been "a Pharisee" as regards the Law (Phil 3:5), they argue
that he is to be understood primarily in the light of his Jewish
heritage. These interpreters draw comparisons between
Paul's exegetical procedures and style of argumentation and
those of Pharisaic and (later) Rabbinic Judaism. They find
numerous allusions to the Old Testament in his letters, even
when Scripture is not specifically cited. They understand
many of his most important theological convictions to be
deeply rooted in the faith of Israel. And they tend to perceive

his ministry as having been guided in various ways by models drawn from Jewish practices current in his day.

Other interpreters, however, insist that Paul, like Pharisaism itself, had been deeply affected by the hellenistic environment, a complex blend of Greek, Roman, and Oriental institutions, customs, and ideals. They observe that he not only wrote his letters in idiomatic Greek, but apparently also read the Scriptures in Greek translation. They argue that Paul himself says nothing about having been formally trained in the Law and that his remark about being unknown to the Jerusalem Christians at the time of his conversion (Gal 1:22) casts doubt on the report in Acts that he had studied there under Gamaliel. They discern numerous parallels between the Apostle's rhetorical style and the conventions of hellenistic rhetoric. They find his preaching to be responsive to many of the general religious interests and longings of his age. And they believe they can locate parallels to many of his social attitudes and specific moral instructions in the traditions of hellenistic popular philosophy.

There is general agreement that this is not an either/or situation. Paul, like most people who lived in the eastern provinces of the Roman Empire, had a diverse cultural heritage. Syncretism, it has been said, was the hallmark of the age. Nevertheless, one's estimate as to whether Paul's Jewish or hellenistic side predominates, or which is primarily operative at this or that specific point, will often substantially influence one's interpretation. This notable instance must suffice as an illustration: When the Apostle expresses his confidence that one day believers will be given a "heavenly dwelling" in place of their present "earthly tent" (2 Cor 4:16–5:5), should his words be interpreted in accord with Jewish expectations about a general resurrection of the dead at the close of history, or in accord with hellenistic conceptions about the immortality of the individual soul? One's opinion about the relative importance of the diverse cultures to which Paul was heir is bound to play some role as one looks for the answer.

Assessing Paul the Man. From time to time modern interpreters, some of them biblical scholars and some not, have sought to discover the kinds of psychic or religious experiences that may have accounted for the extraordinary course of Paul's career and certain aspects of his thought and teachings that are particularly difficult to understand. Such attempts are, to be sure, beset with many difficulties. The investigator has no "clinical evidence" and so must rely entirely on written sources. Although we are fortunate to have access to the subject's own writings, these are relatively few in number, convey very little autobiographical information, contain almost nothing about the Apostle's private religious experiences, and offer only fleeting glimpses of his innermost feelings.

Despite all these difficulties, a few scholars have quite deliberately sought to analyze Paul psychologically, convinced that the results of such an analysis can lead to a better understanding of his ministry and thought.[2] An interpreter must decide whether it is valid and possible to pursue this line of inquiry and, if so, the amount of weight that should be given to the results.

While most scholarly interpreters are hesitant to draw conclusions about Paul's psyche as such, substantial numbers are willing to speculate about the impact of his "conversion experience" on the course of his life and the development of his thought. Doubtless his conversion to

[2]One such older study is D. W. Riddle, *Paul, Man of Conflict: A Modern Biographical Sketch* (Nashville: Cokesbury Press, 1940). See more recently, R. L. Rubenstein, *My Brother Paul* (New York: Harper & Row, 1972).

Christianity marked the decisive turning point in his life. It is
less clear, however, whether the experience itself should be
considered "the key to Pauline theology," as one scholar put
it, and whether the major themes of his preaching are
traceable to the specifics of his Damascus Road encounter,
as the same scholar has suggested.[3] The author of Acts seems
to have been much more interested in the specifics of that
experience (see 9:3-19*a*; 22:6-16; 26:12-18) than was Paul,
whose clearest and fullest reference to it comes, almost
incidentally, in Galatians 1:15-16 (other clear allusions
appear only in 1 Cor 9:1; 15:8). Indeed, while the Acts
accounts may properly be described as "conversion stories,"
Paul himself identifies that experience as a call to
apostleship—or more accurately, as a revelation of the
Christ, for whose service he had been set apart while he was
still in his mother's womb (Gal 1:15). There are two
questions facing interpreters here. First, granting that Paul
understood himself to have been divinely called to
apostleship, is it legitimate to *historicize* that sense of
vocation by postulating, as the accounts in Acts have done,
some specific historical, life-transforming experience?
Second, if one does postulate such an experience, can
enough be known about it to allow any assessment of its
impact on the Apostle's ministry and thought? One's
answers to these questions will affect to some extent one's
interpretation of the Pauline letters.

Identifying the Center of Paul's Gospel. An interpreter
must make a further decision in the process of reading
Pauline texts within their appropriate contexts: What
specific theological convictions give coherence to the
Apostle's thought and teaching? He himself never set forth

[3]See Joachim Jeremias, "The Key to Pauline Theology," *Expository
Times* 76 (1964): 27-30; expanded in *Der Schlüssel zur Theologie des
Apostels Paulus,* Calwer Hefte 115 (Stuttgart: Calwer Verlag, 1971).

any fully comprehensive or systematic exposition of his beliefs. At least there is nothing like that in his surviving letters, although some commentators think that Romans comes close to being such an exposition. Consequently, Paul's interpreters must judge which of his convictions are most basic and therefore most determinative for the overall structure of his theology. Three major options are worth considering.

First, one might identify the theological center of Paul's gospel as "justification by faith," since he was convinced that one cannot be justified by works of the law but only by God's grace. This is how Luther read Paul, and his expositions of the pertinent Pauline texts (e.g., Rom 3:21-31; 5:12-21; the discussions of Abraham in Rom 4 and Gal 3) have continued to exercise a strong influence on interpreters across the centuries. One must acknowledge that there is little or no specific attention given to this theme except in Romans and Galatians. Nevertheless, interpreters who are convinced that it is the focal center of the Apostle's thought argue that it underlies everything he says and that it supplies the broader theological context, even when it is not itself the topic.

As a second possibility, one might understand Paul's theology as centering on what some refer to as a Christ-mysticism, the conviction that the believer's life is intimately bound up with Christ's. One classical exposition from this point of view is Albert Schweitzer's study *The Mysticism of Paul the Apostle,* in which it is argued that Paul's teaching about justification is only "a subsidiary crater, which has formed within the rim of the main center—the mystical doctrine of redemption through the being-in-Christ."[4]

---

[4]Albert Schweitzer, *The Mysticism of Paul the Apostle,* trans. William Montgomery (London: Adam & Charles Black, 1931; 2d ed., 1953; original German ed., 1930), p. 225.

Exemplary of the texts invoked to support this reading of Paul's theology are Galatians 2:19-20 (Christ's indwelling the believer); Romans 6 (baptism into Christ's death); Philippians 3:1-11 (sharing in Christ's suffering, death, resurrection); and the many passages in which the Apostle writes of the believer's life "in Christ."

Still a third possibility is to regard Paul's theology as governed by an essentially "apocalyptic" point of view. This is what J. Christiaan Beker has done in two important books. He argues that all other Pauline themes must be seen in relation to the Apostle's belief in the ultimate victory of the reign of God at the close of history.[5] Those who, like Beker, believe that Paul's gospel is best understood as centered in a cosmicly oriented hope for the future pay special attention to the apocalyptic scenarios of First Corinthians 15, First Thessalonians 4:13-18, and other passages which emphasize that believers are destined to share finally in the glory of God (Rom 5:1-5; 8:15-25; Phil 3:10-11, etc.).

Most interpreters could agree that all three of these doctrines (justification by faith, the life in Christ, the final triumph of God) play some role in Paul's thought and that they are, in fact, somehow interrelated. However, there is no consensus about which, if any, can be identified as the theological center of his gospel. This is one of the decisions each interpreter must make, at least provisionally, if the task of interpretation is to proceed; for every specific Pauline text needs, eventually, to be read within the context of Paul's overall thought.

---

[5]*Paul the Apostle: The Triumph of God in Life and Thought* (Philadelphia: Fortress Press, 1980); *Paul's Apocalyptic Gospel: The Coming Triumph of God* (Philadelphia: Fortress Press, 1982).

III. PAUL INTERPRETED:
THE PAULINE CORPUS

Paul comes to us already interpreted. To be sure, we are in touch with this apostle as with no other first-generation Christian. At the same time, this contact is not as immediate and direct as it appears, because each of Paul's letters is part of a corpus prepared and ordered for church use. The first section of this chapter notes various aspects of this fact and reflects briefly on the consequences for today's interpreter. The second section carries forward the discussion begun in The Scholar's Paul in chapter 2, by showing how the Deutero-Pauline letters themselves deliberately interpret Paul.

The Corpus as Interpreter of Paul

For centuries it was believed that this collection of thirteen letters constitute the literary legacy of Paul; other letters which claimed him as their author—Third Corinthians (now contained in the Acts of Paul), the correspondence between Paul and Seneca, and the Letter to the Laodiceans—were rejected from the canon. Not until modern times did it become evident that the corpus itself contained letters which, with varying degrees of certainty, were not Paul's but the work of his successors (see chapter 1). Our canonical corpus was not the only one, however. In the first half of the second century, an ardent interpreter of Paul provided the movement he fostered with a purely Christian Scripture, containing but the Gospel of Luke and ten epistles of Paul (it lacked the Pastoral Epistles). Moreover, the letters were abbreviated, because the editor, Marcion, believed they had been expanded. Marcion was convinced that Paul's gospel emphasized "freedom from the law" so consistently that the Apostle could not have appealed to the Old Testament for support or have spoken favorably of its God. Yet the Pauline letters being used by the churches at the beginning of the second century did just that. Marcion therefore undertook to purge the letters of what he regarded as secondary elements. Thus the Marcionite churches had access to a "Paul" who differed significantly from the "Paul" of the other churches. The struggle with Marcionism illustrates both how an interpretation of Paul can determine what belongs in the corpus and how the content of the corpus functions as an interpreter of Paul.

Oddly enough, Marcion has his successors in modern criticism, which, for entirely different reasons and for entirely different purposes, also has "reduced" the genuine Paul to the seven uncontested letters, and then, even in those, identified passages that seem to have been added to those Paul himself wrote. Marcion was wrong in *what* he regarded as secondary material, but he was right in thinking that things *had* been added. No one today, of course, proposes to delete either passages or nongenuine letters from the canon.

Unfortunately, no one knows how the corpus came into existence in the first place. Two major possibilities have been advanced. The first infers that the collection was formed

gradually, by accretion, as churches made copies of their
own letters from Paul so they could be shared with Christians
in other cities. The second infers that after a period in which
Paul was neglected, the letters were collected and "published" as a corpus. Indeed, John Knox proposed that it was
Onesimus himself, Philemon's erstwhile runaway slave, who
created the corpus. There is no way such a hypothesis can be
established or disproved, nor is the name of such a
"publisher" of great moment. Basic to this proposal is the
fact that Acts gives the reader no clue that Paul had ever
written letters, and many scholars are convinced that the
author of Acts did not know them. On the whole, viewing the
formation of the corpus as a gradual process creates fewer
problems of historical reconstruction than does seeing it as a
deliberate act to recover Paul after neglect.

In any case, the corpus presents us with an *expanded* Paul
(because it includes the Deutero-Pauline letters), as well as
with an *abbreviated* Paul (because it does not contain
everything Paul wrote; see 1 Cor 5:9) and an *edited* Paul.
This editing appears to have been of two main kinds—one
kind created some of the letters as we now have them, the
other made modifications in what had been created.

The best-known modification of the letters is the deletion
of the reference to Rome in Romans 1:7, 15, which frees this
letter of local particulars. Interestingly, the one Greek
manuscript of Romans which lacks the reference to Rome
provides evidence also that Romans 15–16 was removed, so
that there circulated a form of Romans which consisted of
but 1:1–14:23 (some mss., in fact, have the concluding vv
after 14:23). It is almost certain that Romans 16:25-27 was
added. At Philippians 1:1, the reference to bishops and
deacons looks suspiciously non-Pauline because nowhere
else does Paul mention these officers; suspicious looking
too is "with all those who in every place call on the

name of our Lord Jesus Christ" (1 Cor 1:2), for this turns a letter addressed to the Corinthians into a letter to Christians everywhere. Some additions to the text look as though they were originally marginal comments, which a later copyist mistook for matter that had been omitted but noted, and therefore "restored." For example, Romans 5:6-7 appears to be such a passage, as does Romans 7:25*b*; First Thessalonians 2:14*b*-16 almost certainly was not written by Paul.

Much more important for the interpreter's work is recognizing that editorial work created the letters as we have them. This appears to have been done during the formation of the corpus, because in almost every case the present form of the text is the only one that has come down to us. Critical introductions and commentaries will discuss the evidence in detail, usually under the rubric "Integrity." It should be borne in mind that each proposal to locate a literary seam in a Pauline letter is an effort to account for problems in the text—problems either of transition or of coherence. Both phenomena create difficulties for the interpreter.

Abrupt transitions are easy to identify. The most obvious is in Philippians 3. Verse 1 begins, "Finally . . . rejoice in the Lord"; but verse 2 begins, "Look out for the dogs, look out for the evil-workers," and goes on to develop a polemic throughout the rest of the chapter; at 4:1 the mood changes again. Since chapter 3 is clearly authentic, it is almost certainly part of another of Paul's letters. Furthermore, twice the letter signals its conclusion: "Finally, my brethren . . . " (3:1) and "Finally, brethren . . . " (4:8). It has therefore been proposed that our Philippians combines at least two, if not three letters (4:20-30 + 1:1–3:1; 4:4-7 (21-23?) + 3:2–4:3, 8-9). The abrupt transitions in Second Corinthians also are well known, leading some scholars to find as many as six separate letters represented there.

Rather than attributing unexpected transitions to a change in Paul's mood as he turns to another topic or to a break in dictation, it is preferable to see the hand of an editor who joined parts of different letters.

Problems of coherence are often accompanied by unusual transitions, but they need not be. *Coherence* is a rather elusive criterion, because what one person finds to be inconsistent does not always strike another reader as a problem severe enough to suggest that the text is composite. First Corinthians is the best-known instance of this. For example, in 11:18-19, Paul is rather sanguine about reports of divisions in the Corinthian church, whereas in 1:10-17 and 3:1–4:21, he is intensely critical of factions. Observations such as these have prompted scholars to propose that First Corinthians, too, is a composite letter, though no proposal seems to have achieved a consensus. Indeed, Walter Schmithals believes he has identified six letters to Corinth.[1]

What is the serious student of the Pauline letters to do when confronted by such hypotheses? To begin with, one ought not simply dismiss the whole matter out of hand and seek a scholarly judgment with which one is more comfortable, just as one ought not to accept proposals uncritically because they seem to support a prejudice— "Paul never did make much sense to me." One does, after all, gradually acquire the capacity to assess evidence. Moreover, one ought to be clear about what is and what is not at issue in the discussion. In the case of the Corinthian letters, it is the reconstruction of Paul's relation to Corinth and the development of the crises there that are at stake. Most matters of theological and moral substance do not, finally, rest upon decisions of literary integrity.

[1]Walter Schmithals, *Gnosticism in Corinth* (Nashville: Abingdon Press, 1971), p. 100, n. 30.

Furthermore, being aware of such problems and of proposed solutions should lead one to be circumspect about basing an interpretation on the larger literary context of a given passage. Above all, one begins to appreciate the fact that if a given letter appears to be composite, its editor has already interpreted Paul by the way he put the text together.

An interpretation of Paul is built into both the structure of the corpus and its location in the New Testament. The corpus has a simple structure: Letters to churches come before those to persons; among the latter, those to associates stand ahead of that to a friend, Philemon. Above all, the letters are not placed in the sequence in which they were written. Were that the case, the list would begin with First Thessalonians and end with Romans, assuming that none of the Philippian correspondence originated in Caesarea or in Rome. The sequence in our New Testament is the one that came to prevail over others, such as those in the following lists.

Marcion	Canon Muratori	Codex Claromontanus	Athanasius
Gal	1 Cor	Rom	Rom
1 Cor	2 Cor	1 Cor	1 Cor
2 Cor	Eph	2 Cor	2 Cor
Rom	Phil	Gal	Gal
1 Thess	Col	Eph	Eph
2 Thess	Gal	1 Tim	Phil
Eph	1 Thess	2 Tim	Col
Col	2 Thess	Titus	1 Thess
Phil	Rom	Col	2 Thess
		Phlm	Heb
			1 Tim
			2 Tim
			Titus
			Phlm

It is instructive to recall that E. J. Goodspeed argued that
Ephesians was written as an "introduction" to the original
Pauline corpus ("like the overture of an opera, fore-
shadowing the melodies that are to follow"[2]). Were this
valid, we would have four portals to the House of Paul:
Ephesians as a resumé, Galatians as the anti-Law key
signature, First and Second Corinthians as the most widely
cited texts, and Romans as a treatise on the gospel.
Moreover, Goodspeed suggested that the order of Marcion's
list was that of the original collection, except that he placed
Galatians first and Ephesians where Galatians had been. In
that case, the original sequence would have been based on
length (counting the letters to Corinth and Thessalonica as
units), although this hypothesis cannot be established. The
point here, however, is a simple one: The sequence of letters
is a deliberate way of presenting Paul; it incorporates an
interpretation of those that are deemed most important.
Even today, scholars commonly speak of the *first* four as the
big four.

The placement of the Pauline corpus within our New
Testament canon is also significant: It follows Acts and
comes before the Catholic Epistles. In this location, together
with Acts, Paul certainly dominates the New Testament,
thereby implying that he was, in fact, the most important
figure in the first-century church. However, this customary
placement was not the only one known in antiquity.
According to a number of ancient manuscripts, as well as the
Canon of the Council of Laodicea (A.D. 360), the Easter letter
of Athanasius (A.D. 367)—the oldest list whose content is
identical with the New Testament we use—the Catholic
epistles precede the Pauline corpus. This placement suggests

[2]Goodspeed, *An Introduction to the New Testament* (Chicago: University
of Chicago Press, 1937), p. 227.

that what is "Catholic" takes precedence over what is "Pauline," not the reverse.

Paul's Earliest Interpreters

Strictly speaking, Paul's earliest interpreters were those individuals and groups who, during his own lifetime, heard him preach, received his instructions and counsel, and were in dialogue with him about matters of mutual concern. Those earliest interpreters would also have included his associates in ministry—Silvanus, Timothy, Titus, and others—who were part of his apostolic entourage and who, on occasion, were commissioned by Paul to represent him where he could not be present (e.g., the missions of Timothy to Thessalonica [1 Thess 3:2-3] and of Titus to Corinth [2 Cor 7:5-16]). Of course, Paul's rivals and opponents such as those he faced in Galatia and Corinth were also "interpreters" of his ministry and gospel, even though, from the Apostle's point of view, they seriously *mis*interpreted him.

Apart from the Pauline letters themselves, however, we have little information about the Apostle's *very* earliest interpreters. Those of whom we have direct knowledge are the several other New Testament writers who were either directly or indirectly acquainted with his ministry and sought in some way to represent it or to comment on it. One such person was the anonymous author of Luke-Acts; another was the writer who, using Peter's name, remarked on the difficulty of understanding Paul's letters and the readiness with which they could be used by false teachers (2 Pet 3:15-16). Sometimes the discussion of faith and works in James 2:14-26 is read as an interpretation (or "correction") of Paul, and if so, that writer too might be listed among the early interpreters, though the Apostle's name is not specifically introduced. However, the most important early interpreters with whom we have direct contact are those admirers of the Apostle who were responsible for the Deutero-Pauline letters. It is with those interpreters that we are concerned here, because they actually wrote in Paul's name and because their work came to be included in the Pauline corpus.

We believe, along with many other scholars, that our New Testament contains six Deutero-Pauline letters: Second Thessalonians, Colossians, Ephesians, and the three Pastorals—First and Second Timothy, and Titus. Several considerations lead us to this conclusion.

1. There are numerous differences in form, function, style, vocabulary, and theological point of view between these letters and the ones that are certainly Paul's.

2. In at least one case (2 Thess) there is clear literary dependence on the Apostle's own writing.

3. Certain issues and situations addressed in these letters do not correspond with those Paul is likely to have confronted during his lifetime.

4. It is virtually impossible to fit some of these letters (notably the Pastorals) into the chronology which seems to be required by the letters known to be authentic.

These matters, which must be addressed letter by letter, are considered in detail by the better commentaries (see those mentioned in "Aids for the Interpreter"), and some will be illustrated in chapter 5 as we examine specific Deutero-Pauline texts.

Once these writings have been removed from the list of "authentic" Pauline letters, what is one to do with them? Can one nevertheless use them for preaching and for teaching *as if* they were Paul's own? Or must they be dismissed as forgeries and, in effect, excluded from our canon? Are their authors to be regarded as pious cheats who masqueraded as the Apostle in order to gain a hearing for their own ideas? As persons intent on infiltrating the developing Pauline tradition with alien understandings of what faith is and requires? When one considers such questions, several things need to be borne in mind.

First, it would be a mistake to impose upon the ancient world our modern ideas about legitimate and illegitimate claims to authorship. That a person may own "intellectual property," an idea fundamental to all modern copyright laws, seems to have played little or no role in ancient literary production.[3] Moreover, the phenomenon of pseudonymity— representing a writing as that of another person—was not uncommon in the ancient world.

Second, it should be noted that there were different kinds of pseudonymous works. Where there was a clear intent to deceive or to defraud, one certainly spoke of a forgery, and that was condemned. But other instances of pseudonymity occurred when anonymous works were wrongly attributed, when copyists made mistakes, or when, within a particular intellectual or religious tradition, the names of revered leaders or teachers from the past were attached to the community's most important literature.

Third, and with special reference to the last-mentioned type of pseudonymity, it is important to recognize that by the end of the first century, the martyred Peter and Paul were being identified as Christian apostles par excellence, and their names could be invoked to represent the apostolic tradition as a whole. Thus Clement of Rome, writing near the year 96, referred to them as "the perfect and most righteous pillars of the Church" (*1 Clem* 5:2) and regarded them as the guarantors of the tradition he commended to his readers (e.g., 42:1-5; 44:1-2). The writing that stands in the

[3]The phrase is used by K. Koch, "Pseudonymous Writing," in *The Interpreter's Dictionary of the Bible,* Suppl. Vol. (Nashville: Abingdon Press, 1976), pp. 712-14.

New Testament as "Second Peter," certainly not written by that apostle and very likely dated as late as the middle of the second century, is a clear case of the name of a venerated apostle having been used to certify Christian teaching that a later writer firmly believed to be correct.

The reference to Paul in Second Peter 3:15-16 suggests yet a fourth matter one needs to bear in mind in approaching the Deutero-Pauline letters. Because Paul's own letters could be interpreted in different ways, they could also be *mis*interpreted and used in ways contrary to the Apostle's intentions and to the apostolic tradition in general. Therefore one of the church's concerns after Paul's death was to guard that tradition by counteracting perceived misinterpretations of the Pauline letters with interpretations deemed more appropriate.

Finally, it may be observed that the church experienced (and still experiences) difficulty in interpreting the letters, largely because they were so situation-specific (see above, pp. 20-21). Because the apostle had been addressing, for the most part, topics and issues related to the particular needs of local congregations, later Christians, more or less removed from those situations, required help in understanding the meaning of Paul's words for their lives. They were experiencing conditions the Apostle had not experienced and confronting decisions he and his converts never found it necessary to make.

These few observations about pseudonymous writing in the ancient world, the status in the church of the martyred Paul, and the church's need to interpret and adapt Paul's teaching to new conditions provide the needed clues for at least a general understanding of the origin and function of the Deutero-Pauline letters. They originated, doubtless, in circles where the Pauline tradition was especially honored. They represent the attempt of different anonymous writers within those circles to adapt Paul's teaching to later times and circumstances, or to counteract what they took to be the misuse of his letters by teachers who held positions contrary to their own. One suspects that for the communities in and for which the Deutero-Paulines were produced, the important thing was not "who wrote them," but that they brought the apostolic tradition into touch with current needs. Therefore each of these letters must be read, first of all, in the context of its own time and place, with an appreciation for the situation that called it forth. While it is certainly appropriate to consider how perceptively a given writer interpreted Paul and whether that writer respected the fundamental tenets of Paul's gospel, such considerations should not distract from the primary task, which is to understand how *that* writer, addressing *those* issues, sought to represent the gospel to *those* readers.

The author of *Colossians,* for example, was concerned with pointing out the errors of a certain false "philosophy" (2:8) being propagated, evidently in the Lycus valley region of Asia Minor. While the exact nature of that errant teaching is unclear, it seems to have involved some kind of special regard for what the author refers to as "the elemental spirits of the universe." It may be that these should be understood as cosmic powers of some kind. In any case, the author warns that veneration of these "spirits" (if that is what is going on) is a denial of the cosmic lordship of Christ. As a consequence, the major theme of this letter is Christ's status as Lord of the universe and the conduct required of the believer who, through baptism, has died to those "elemental spirits" and been raised above with Christ (see, e.g., 2:20–3:4).

It has been estimated that more than half the contents of Colossians is reflected, more or less directly, in *Ephesians.* Not only are certain ideas held in common and certain of the same topics addressed, but there are even parallels in wording, some so close that one of these authors must have known and used the work of the other. Scholars are now generally agreed that it was the author of Ephesians who used Colossians. In the later writing, the cosmic Christology of Colossians has been carried over, but it is now assimilated to the special purpose of Ephesians: to affirm and praise the glory and unity of the church under Christ's lordship and to summon all believers to conduct themselves in ways appropriate to their "one hope . . . one Lord, one faith, one baptism, one God and Father" (4:4-6). Since the best manuscripts make no reference to Ephesus in the salutation (1:1), it is probable that the author was addressing Christians in general, and this seems to be confirmed by the nonspecific way in which the all-pervasive theme of Christian unity is developed. What we have here, then, is not really "a letter to Ephesus"; it is more like a theological tractate addressed to the church at large.

If, as we are suggesting, *Second Thessalonians* is also to be regarded as Deutero-Pauline, it would be the only writing in this category specifically addressed to a congregation that had received one of the Apostle's own letters. Just as the parallels between Colossians and Ephesians suggest that the latter was dependent upon the former, so the parallels between First and Second Thessalonians (it is estimated that about one-third of 2 Thess consists of sentences and expressions found as well in 1 Thess) suggest that Paul's own letter was closely followed by the later writer. Despite many similarities, however, there is a major difference in point of view between First and Second Thessalonians. Whereas in First Thessalonians 5:1-3 it is emphasized that "the day of the Lord" (Christ's return, the resurrection of the dead, and the gathering up of all believers to be "with the Lord" [4:16-17]) will come suddenly and without warning, in

Second Thessalonians (2:3-4, 7-12) it is emphasized that various specific historical events must precede the Lord's return and will therefore clearly signal the day. It would appear that Second Thessalonians was written in order to oppose the view of some Christians, perhaps based on their misinterpretation of First Thessalonians, that "the day of the Lord has come" (2 Thess 2:2). It has even been suggested that this author has First Thessalonians in mind when the readers are warned not to be "excited . . . by [a] letter purporting to be from us." If this is so, then one would have to understand Second Thessalonians as written in order to replace one of the genuinely Pauline letters in order to prevent that from being misinterpreted.

Finally, the *Pastoral Epistles* (1 and 2 Tim, and Titus) may be considered together, since they certainly are the work of the same author. A good overall statement of his purpose (the author is undoubtedly a man, see 1 Tim 2:12) is found in First Timothy 3:14b-15: "I am writing these instructions to you so that . . . you may know how one ought to behave in the household of God." More specifically, this author is concerned with counteracting certain kinds of beliefs and practices which he believes are not only destructive of the fabric of Christian community, but which also place the whole Christian community at risk in its dealings with outsiders (see, e.g., 1 Tim 2:1-2; Titus 2).

While the Pastorals outwardly conform to the pattern of a typical Pauline letter, they have been composed in such a way as to suggest a great teacher recording for his pupils (Timothy and Titus), and thus for all posterity, a "last will and testament" which summarizes the legacy of his own life's work. The writer stresses, above all, the need for Christians to conduct themselves according to the ideal of *eusebeia,* variously translated in the Revised Standard Version as "godliness" or "religion." This is a specifically hellenistic virtue (there is no equivalent Hebrew word), akin to what we might think of as *piety, reverence,* or simple *respect.* It is listed along with "righteousness . . . faith, love, steadfastness, gentleness" as one of the virtues to which the "man of God" should aspire (1 Tim 6:11) and seems to be thought of as all-inclusive, as when Timothy is admonished, "Train yourself in godliness; for while bodily training is of some value, godliness is of value in every way, as it holds promise for the present life and also for the life to come" (1 Tim 4:7*b*-8).

The Pastoral Epistles may have been written as late as 125. Colossians and Ephesians are presumably from the last decades of the first century—certainly after Paul's death in the early 60s and probably before the time of Ignatius (early second century), whose letters seem to reflect an acquaintance with Ephesians. It is possible that Second Thessalonians was composed about the same time.

IV. PAUL AS INTERPRETER

Paul's letters are literary precipitates of his need to interpret the gospel he had preached. They are not the results of his drive to express himself, since he was not an "author," nor could he ever have introduced himself as a "writer." He wrote these letters because he became convinced that he had to interpret his gospel, lest alternate interpretations of it prevail in his churches. In this chapter we will watch Paul at work interpreting texts, traditions, themes, situations, practices. His creativity manifests itself in his capacity to interpret. In retrospect, one can say that he created something new, but it is not as a creator, or originator, of "new theology" that he understood himself.

This discussion will proceed in the explanatory mode rather than undertake an interpretation of Paul; the purpose is to facilitate interpretation, not to prescribe procedures for it. Besides, there are rules for explanation, but none for interpretation. Perceptive interpreters do not "follow rules"; those who do are more likely to be mechanics than interpreters. One reason for watching Paul at work is to learn from a master.

Paul is a coherent writer but not a systematic one. Consequently he does not discuss topics in a logically ordered sequence. Instead, foundational ideas are sometimes stated in passing, practical consequences are pointed out before principles are formulated, and matters important for *our* understanding are assumed. But then, Paul was not writing to us but, apart from the Letter to the Romans, to people who already had heard him. What we need to ascertain, he could assume or mention only in passing. To watch Paul interpret, moreover, is to observe him weaving together ethics and Christology, interpretation of texts and interpretation of readers, into statements whose theological density requires rigorous thought and disciplined historical imagination to unfold. The Pauline letters have no fluff and few throw-away lines. Learning from Paul is not a matter of imitating his style or his method, but of discerning, from case to case, what interpretation involves so that one may the better undertake it oneself.

Given Paul's way of weaving themes together, any attempt to classify his interpretive work entails a certain arbitrariness. It is essentially for the sake of convenience that the passages will be grouped under four rubrics: Paul as interpreter of the Christ-event, of ethical traditions, of the experience of the Spirit, and of Scripture.

Paul as Interpreter of the Christ-event

Paul was not an interpreter of the teachings and deeds of Jesus, but of the event called "Jesus Christ." Never does he mention even a single incident in Jesus' life, other than his execution; his relatively rare interpretations of Jesus' teaching will be discussed in the next section. The range of Paul's knowledge of the traditions about Jesus remains disputed, as does the extent to which he previously had included them in his preaching and teaching. One may infer that Paul actually was more interested in "the historical Jesus" than his letters indicate, given the fact that they are by no means resumés of his thought, but inference is not evidence. In any case, Paul interpreted the event called Jesus Christ as being decisive—for the human condition, for our knowledge of God, for an appropriate way of life, and for the future of the world. In developing his interpretation of Christ, he never appeals to anything that Jesus said about these themes.

The place to begin our discussion is where Paul himself said he began—with the tradition of Jesus' death and resurrection (1 Cor 15:3-7). Interestingly enough, First Corinthians 15 is an instructive instance of Paul's way of weaving together precisely the four themes noted above! This is one of the two times Paul says he is quoting a tradition (the other being 1 Cor 11:23-25), though we shall see that he does so also elsewhere, but without calling attention to it. The tradition may be set out as follows (RSV adapted):

> That Christ died for our sins
>   in accordance with the Scriptures
> That he was buried
> That he was raised on the third day
>   in accordance with the Scriptures
> And that he appeared to Cephas
>   then to the Twelve.
>   Then he appeared to more than 500 brethren at one time (most of whom are still alive, though some have fallen asleep).
>   Then he appeared to James
>   then to all the apostles.

Paul not only inserted the comment in parentheses, but added himself to this tradition: "Last of all, as to one untimely born, he appeared also to me." This addition allowed him to write verses 9-11, in which he defends his apostleship in relation to other apostles. He rounds off this paragraph by bringing the reader back to the point of departure:

vv 1-2   I want you to know, brethren, in what terms I
          preached to you the gospel [literally, "the gospel
          which I gospeled you"], which you received, in
          which you stand, by which you are being saved, if
          you hold it fast—unless you believed in vain.

v 11   Whether then it was I or they, so we preach and so
          you believed.

The rest of the chapter unfolds the meaning both of this tradition and of the Corinthians' acceptance of it. This whole discussion was evoked by the fact that some Corinthians, doubtless including some who had heard Paul directly, were now saying, "There is no resurrection of the dead." It is likely that for them this was not a "counsel of despair" but a triumphant assertion.

• Here we note the importance of explanation for understanding: To understand the Corinthian assertion, one must
explain how they could have come to this point of view, and
this entails reconstructing their interpretation of the same
tradition. Paul interprets the tradition into that specific
situation. Genuine interpretation always occurs into an
actual context, where meaning reoccurs.

• Meaning is not a thing, nor is it simply "there" waiting to be
exposed, like a vein of coal. Rather, meaning is an event, a
transaction between text (or tradition) and the reader. The
interpreter brings the meaning to pass and so is a sort of
midwife who assists in the birth of meaning.

• What resurrection "means" depends on the situation into which it is being interpreted.

The Corinthians neither repudiated the tradition nor denied that Jesus had been raised (what was denied is "resurrection of the dead" [*anastasis nekrōn*]). Thus they apparently made two interpretive moves: They took resurrection to mean resuscitation, a resumption of life as currently known; and they seem to have interpreted the raising of Jesus as the "elevation" of his released spirit so that it could return to its otherworldly origin. Manifestly, they had interpreted the resurrection-gospel into the dualistic mentality of the Greco-Roman world, according to which salvation consisted of releasing the soul (or spirit) from its bodily prison. Later, Gnostics would pick up the old slogan Sōma-Sēma ("body-tomb"). One reason Paul is able to interpret the resurrection into the Corinthians' "semantic universe" is that he agrees with them on one fundamental point: "Flesh and blood cannot inherit the kingdom of God, nor does the perishable inherit the imperishable" (1 Cor 15:50). Their solution is release from "flesh and blood"; Paul's is to deny that resurrection is resuscitation (that the perishable simply becomes imperishable) and to insist instead that resurrection means transformation ("We shall all be changed" vv 51-54). At the moment of resurrection, both the living and the dead will be transmuted into another mode of being, which Paul calls the spiritual body (v 44). Paul had already prepared for this point by arguing that there *are* different modes of bodily being (vv 35-41), of which the resurrection-body is an instance (vv 42-49).

• Apt interpretation occurs when the interpreter is able to commute between two worlds of thought. Interpretation is not a substitute for theological reflection and explanation, but often precipitates them.

Paul interprets not only the resurrection but also the Corinthian interpretation of it (vv 12-19). In doing so, he does not argue against the dualistic mentality itself, for (as noted) he grants that its essential point is correct. Rather he interprets the consequences of their interpretation—that is, he exposes its contradiction as being so great that it actually self-destructs. Again he shares common ground, though it is not expressed: What happened to Christ will happen to Christians as well. The Corinthians seem to have taken this to mean that baptism had made them participants in Christ's resurrection so that their experiences of the Spirit were regarded as anticipations of release from the body (see section on Paul as Interpreter of the Spirit). They also may have regarded dying as calling into question the validity of Paul's gospel. Paul, however, insists that Christ is "the first fruits of those who have fallen asleep," a statement he proceeds to explain: For Christians, the "being made alive" must await the coming of Christ. Death is the *last* enemy to be destroyed. Christians, like everyone else, still must die (vv 20-26). If there is no resurrection of the dead, then there is hope only for the living, not for the dead (vv 18-19). But if this is the case, why do the Corinthians practice vicarious baptism on behalf of the dead (vv 29-30)? This practice (mentioned only here and apparently practiced only in Corinth and only in Paul's day) contradicts their own interpretation. Moreover, Paul points out that the raising of Christ and the resurrection of Christians stand or fall together (v 13), so the latter cannot be denied without denying the former. In addition, he exposes the contradiction between the view the Corinthians now hold and the view they came to hold in order to become Christians—"If Christ is not raised, your faith is futile and you are still in your sins."

● The faith that makes one a Christian is not a threshold to be crossed, after which one may reinterpret the gospel without affecting one's status vis-à-vis that gospel. What claims to be interpretation might be forfeiture.

The tradition had already interpreted Jesus' execution as Christ's death "for our sins in accordance with the scriptures." That is, it was neither a miscarriage of justice nor a heroic martyrdom for a cause, but an event that dealt effectively with "our" sins—an open-ended phrase which includes everyone who accepts the tradition. It is as useless to speculate on exactly which Scriptures are in view (though some think of Isa 53) as it is to define exactly what theory of the atonement is implied in the phrase "for our sins." This tradition is concerned not with explanation, but with confession. Those who recited it acknowledged themselves to be the beneficiaries of Christ's death—that their sins had been dealt with definitively, so that they now stood in a new relationship to God and to one another.

● An interpreter respects the "intent" of the text, including its scope, and guards against "over-interpretation."

● An interpreter can disengage a tradition from its present context in order to reflect on its content, its rationale in the life of the community of faith.

● The fact that Paul interprets only the resurrection part of the tradition does not require also today's interpreter to ignore the first part.

In *Romans 3:21-26* Paul interprets another piece of tradition, which provides the explanation absent from First Corinthians 15:3-7. This passage (one cumbersome relentless sentence) inaugurates the second part of the argument begun at Romans 1:18. The first part indicts humanity (first the Gentile, then the Jew) and reaches its climax not only in the assertion that the whole world is culpable before God, but also in the claim that "no human being will be justified . . . by works of the law since through the law comes knowledge of sin" (3:20). Paul postpones explaining the role of the Law and proceeds to develop the gospel's alternative to the human plight. To do so, he picks up the theme of God's righteousness which he had announced at 1:17: "For in it [the gospel] the righteousness of God is revealed through faith for faith." Now he formulates the theme again:

> But now the righteousness of God is manifested apart from the law, although the law and the prophets bear witness to it, the righteousness of God through faith in Jesus Christ for all who believe. For there is no distinction; since all have sinned and fall short of the glory of God, they are justified by his grace as a gift, through the redemption which is in Christ Jesus, whom God put forward as an expiation by his blood, to be received by faith. This was to show God's righteousness, because in his divine forbearance he had passed over former sins; it was to prove at the present time that he himself is righteous and that he justifies [rectifies] the one who has faith in Jesus. (RSV adapted)

It is doubtful whether anyone can even punctuate this sentence properly. Even if one regards verses 22*b*-23 ("for there is no distinction . . . glory of God") as a parenthesis, verse 24 not only switches to a different subject but begins the sentence all over again and forgets to include a main verb. This may well result from Paul's adopting a fragment of a tradition, which causes him to garble the syntax because he concentrates so intently on what he is trying to say. It is regrettable that there is no consensus about the exact wording of the tradition. Probably it included phrases with vocabulary not found elsewhere in Paul—in other words, the tradition is contained in verses 25-26*a* ("whom God put forward . . . former sins"). For our purposes, the matter need not be pursued further since our focus of concern is the phrase "whom God put forward as a *hilastērion.*"

The word *hilastērion* is used only here by Paul. One possible meaning is *mercy seat,* as in Hebrews 9:5. The mercy seat was the lid of the Ark of the Covenant, the sacred box in "the Holy of Holies," the heart of the Hebrews' tabernacle and later of the Temple. The high priest entered this inner room but once a year (on the Day of Atonement), to sprinkle the mercy seat with sacrificial blood in order to consummate this ritual which atoned for the people's sins. On this basis, the tradition would say that God "put forward" Christ as the mercy seat—the place where atonement was made. The other possible meaning of the word is much less specific—*expiation.* Expiation is not to be confused with propitiation. The latter refers to something that placates divine wrath; the former refers to something that expunges human sin. Propitiation changes the divine attitude; expiation changes the human condition. The Revised Standard Version is almost certainly correct in rendering *hilastērion* as *expiation.* On this basis, the tradition would say that God put forward Christ as a sacrifice in order to deal with human sin.

For ancients, this way of speaking of Christ's death needed little explanation, because for centuries Greeks, no less than Jews, assumed that blood sacrifice was an effective remedy for sin. This is why the tradition could simply assert "expiation by his blood." One interesting feature of the Epistle to the Hebrews can now be appreciated. Hebrews 9 also discusses Christ's death in sacrificial categories, but insists that animal sacrifices cannot purify the human conscience; only Christ's sacrifice of himself can do that. But even Hebrews reaffirms the principle: "Without shedding of blood there is no forgiveness of sins" (9:22). In other words, Hebrews and the tradition used in Romans 3:25 stand in a tradition which sees in "blood" (equals sacrificed life) power to deal with sin.

But since human sacrifice was an abomination in Jewish thought, how did Paul's tradition come to regard the death of Christ as a sacrifice which expiates sin? Is there a precedent in the Jewish tradition? Interestingly enough, there is a hellenistic Jewish text, probably written shortly after Paul became a Christian—that is, about the same time this tradition would have been formed—which uses the precise word *hilastērion* when referring to human death. This text is Fourth Maccabees, which celebrates the heroism of Jewish martyrs during the persecution by Antiochus Epiphanes IV (168–165 BCE). According to the old legend, seven brothers were tortured, yet remained faithful unto death. Near the end of the gruesome story, the author writes that they became "as a ransom for the sin of the nation. It was through the blood of these righteous ones, and through the expiation [*hilastērion*] of their death, that divine Providence preserved Israel" (17:22). In other words, the voluntary death of the martyrs was accepted by God as an atonement for sin. There is no reason to think that the Christian community in which Paul's tradition was formed had read Fourth Maccabees. What this parallel does provide, however, is evidence that in Jewish thought of the time, it was possible to speak of human execution as expiation for sin.

The Christian tradition, however, goes beyond Fourth Maccabees. In the latter, God accepts the martyrs' deaths as expiation after the fact; according to the former, God undertook to provide the expiatory death—to put forward Christ. This is an altogether remarkable interpretation, for it not only views the Christ-event from the standpoint of its outcome—execution—but asserts that it was God's deed for the sake of human sin. Clearly, this tradition agrees fully with the more simple formulation of First Corinthians 15:3—"that Christ died for our sins." It is also of a piece with another formula which states that Jesus "was put to death for our trespasses and raised for our justification" (Rom 4:25). In short, Paul accepts the traditions that interpret Jesus' death in terms of sacrifice which deals effectively with sin.

At the same time, he interprets the tradition in a way that is both characteristic of Paul and remarkable in its own right. In contrast with Hebrews, which further develops the logic of Christ as sacrifice, Paul shows virtually no interest in reflecting on the sacrifice itself, nor does his interpretation of Jesus' death rely on the vocabulary of the cultus. His interest lies not in unfolding the meaning of *hilastērion,* but in the implications of the word *proetheto*—"put [him] forward." Moreover, in Romans 3:25-26 he connects this with God's righteousness in the face of the universal human culpability which he had exposed in Romans 1:18–3:20. There is no reason to think that Paul was critical of *hilastērion* thinking; after all, he was not required to cite it. Yet he was free to emphasize something else and to interpret that.

Paul's interest in interpreting God's "putting forward" of Christ shows up elsewhere in Romans. In Romans 5:8 he interprets the point in his own words: "God shows his love for us in that while we were yet sinners Christ died for us." This is Paul's Christology in a nutshell: *Christ's* death "for us" is an act of *God's* love which confronts humanity "while we were yet sinners." Christ's death as God's deed is wholly undeserved by humanity; it is motivated solely by God's love, and it is possible only if God is free to relate to sinful humanity on terms other than "cause and effect," only if God is not the heavenly paymaster who metes out exactly what everyone deserves. Paul the interpreter took the tradition's wording so seriously that he thought its logic through to the end. Thereby he grasped the import of the tradition for the whole of humanity: The grace of God effects justification. That, in short, is the christological pivot of the letter to the Romans.

To show how Paul interprets God's "putting forward" Christ in relation to the righteousness of God would lead to rehearsing the argument of virtually the whole of Romans. Here the scope must be much more modest, and the following apodictical statements must suffice.

1. God's righteousness is God's character, God's moral integrity, God's rectitude, God's self-fidelity—especially in view of human infidelity (see Rom 3:3-4).

2. Wherever God's integrity or rectitude expresses itself according to Law, there God's rectitude undergirds the maxim "You get what you deserve," as in Psalm 1. This simple straightforward theology leads Job's friends to reverse the argument: Job must have done something wrong, otherwise he would not be in such misery.

3. If God's rectitude expresses itself "apart from law" (Rom 3:21), then the Law's nexus of achievement/reward is not the base on which to understand God's intergrity. But can one speak of God's rectitude "apart from law," independent of Moses? Indeed, if God's response to the human condition is the "putting forward" of Christ, then the Christ-event cannot be understood within the framework of Law-rectitude. As a matter of fact, in Galatians 3, Paul again interprets the "putting forward" tradition—"Christ became a curse for us" by being crucified, because the Law of Moses pronounces, in God's name, a curse on "everyone who hangs on a tree" (Gal 3:13). If God vindicated and exalted Jesus by resurrecting him (and him only) from the realm of the dead, then obviously the Law cannot tell us reliably about the event of Jesus; rather, in the light of the resurrection, it is the Christ-event that tells us reliably about the Law. In short, if

"God shows his love for us in that while we were yet sinners Christ died for us," then God's integrity, God's rectitude, asserts itself not in punishing the sinner but in taking the initiative to set things right. Then God's rectitude rectifies. It is this rationale that Paul expresses when he interprets the "putting forth" as a demonstration of God's rectitude—"So that he might be righteous and rectify (RSV: "justify") the one who believes in Jesus" (Rom 3:26). In short, apart from Law, God is the one who "justifies the ungodly" (Rom 4:5). For Paul, justification means rectification of the relationship to God, a rectification made possible because God seized the initiative and manifested divine rectitude and love in "putting forth" Christ "while we were yet sinners." In short, Paul interprets the tradition as justification.

4. Finally, this divine freedom to initiate a new rectified relation to God is consonant with the real meaning of Scripture ("the law and the prophets bear witness to it"). Thus Paul undertakes a fresh interpretation of Scripture, and of the call of Israel. The inherited way of interpreting both is recast in light of what God has done in the Christ-event. This will be explored later in the section on Paul as Interpreter of Scripture.

● What has the cursory discussion of two passages, First Corinthians and Romans 3:21-26, shown us about Paul the interpreter that is instructive for today's interpretive work? First, no interpretation begins at zero-point; rather, all interpretation stands within a stream of interpretation, explicit or tacit. Second, today's interpreter, too, inherits a way of reading the texts, not simply Catholic or Protestant, liberal or conservative, but shaped by assumptions about a nonnegotiable starting point. For Paul, it was the death-resurrection of Jesus; if one does not share Paul's Archimedean fulcrum, one must find another. Finally, if interpretation is to be consistent and coherent, and not merely ad hoc, it will lead one to theological reflection on the whole fabric of the Christian faith.

Another type of christological tradition is found in *Galatians 4:4-6*, which is part of a complex argument begun at 3:1. Given the Galatian trend toward accepting circumcision, Paul insists that "every man who receives circumcision . . . is bound to keep the whole law" (5:3). Law, however, is precisely that structure of the God/human relationship from which Christ has freed believers. True, "the law was our guardian [RSV's "custodian" suggests a janitor] until Christ came. . . . But now that faith has come [i.e., a structure of the God/human relationship] we are no longer under a guardian, for in Christ Jesus you are all sons of God, through faith" (3:24-26). The word for "guardian" is *paidagōgos,* the "tutor" under whose authority a child was placed until coming to maturity. Paul was not interpreting the Law of Moses as that which educates one into Christ, but as a structure of authority under which one lives until adulthood (here, being a "son," no longer a child). The Galatians, of course, had never lived under the jurisdiction of the Law of Moses; they were Gentiles. Yet they too had lived under a structure of authority and obligation—the *stoicheia tou kosmou* (RSV: "the elemental spirits of the universe" [4:3]), the hierarchy of invisible powers to which they had been beholden. Thus Paul interprets the situation of Gentile and Jew, before coming to faith in Christ, as lack of freedom, being under the control of a structure of obligation, being a "child" rather than a "son." Becoming a Christian was therefore an emancipation from being a ward of the court, so to speak. For the Gentile to accept circumcision, and thereby to obligate himself to obey the whole Law, is nothing less than a relapse (3:9).

To develop this argument Paul relies on a tradition, or at least a traditional train of thought. One can infer this from the fact that Romans 8:1-17 and Galatians 4:3-6 have the same sequence of themes and phrases:

Romans	*Galatians*
the sending of the Son	the sending of the Son
the receipt of the Spirit	the sending of the Spirit
sonship	sonship
Abba	Abba

These are the only places in which Paul refers to the Christian prayer as Abba (Father). Both Galatians and Romans, each in its own way, interpret the traditional sequence of ideas.

The wording of the tradition itself is not altogether clear. On the one hand, it is possible that to the tradition which said that God "sent out" the Son (from heaven) to be "born of woman so that we might receive adoption as sons," Paul added "born under the law to redeem those who were under the law." On this basis, Paul interprets the sending of the Son of God as the birth of Jesus as a Jew in order to redeem people from the guardianship of the Law so that they may become "sons." On the other hand, if "born under the law" was part of the tradition, the tradition might have read: "God sent forth his Son, born of woman, born under the law, so that we might receive adoption as sons." On this basis, Paul would have reinterpreted the force of the tradition drastically by inserting "to redeem those who were under the law," making sonship depend not upon fulfilling the Law, as this form of the tradition could be taken, but on being redeemed from it. It is difficult to decide which is the more likely. In either case, here the Christ-event itself is spoken of from the standpoint of its "origin," on the one hand, and of its salvific intent, on the other. Furthermore, the ecstatic "Abba!" attests to the sonship—to the liberation from the *paidagōgos,* be it Moses or the *stoicheia.* (There is insufficient evidence to conclude that "Abba!" alludes to the Lord's Prayer.)

Nowhere else does Paul write so negatively about the Law. Here he does so because he sees in the Galatian situation something the Galatians themselves do not see—that it cannot be the intent of the Christ-event to produce a situation in which the relation to God depends upon fulfilling a structure of obligations; for both Jews and Gentiles—each group in its own way—had been in that situation before. In the nonpolemical situation of Romans, Paul can write that God's aim in sending the Son was "that the just requirement of the law might be fulfilled in us, who walk . . . according to the Spirit" (Rom 8:4).

> • Interpretation is not a soliloquy, addressed to no one in particular; rather it effects meaning by releasing the perceived import of the text into a specific situation. Interpreting a text entails interpreting the situation well. Since circumcision among Gentile Christians today has no religious significance whatever, understanding and interpreting Paul's views in Galatians entails discerning a current equivalent.

The best-known Pauline interpretation of a christological tradition is found in *Philippians 2.* Although there is broad agreement that in verses 6-11 Paul cites an early Christian hymn, discussion continues about most details. There is broad consensus that "even death on a cross" is Paul's own comment. There is also agreement that the hymn has two parts, verses 6-8 and 9-11: In the first, Christ is the subject of the verbs; in the second, it is God who acts. In this context it is not necessary to adjudicate different attempts to recover the original versification; it suffices to set out the hymn (RSV adapted):

> Who being in the form of God
> did not count equality with God something to be grasped
> but emptied himself
> taking the form of a slave
> occurring in the likeness of men.
> And being found in human form
> he humbled himself
> becoming obedient to death
>   [even death on a cross].
>
> Therefore God has highly exalted him
> and bestowed on him the name which is above every name
> that at the name of Jesus every knee should bow
> in heaven and on earth and under the earth
> and every tongue confess that Jesus Christ is Lord
> to the glory of God the Father.

The most important decision the exegete must make is whether the hymn celebrates the Christ-event by beginning with preexistence before speaking of the incarnation, or whether it celebrates it by portraying Christ's action as the antithesis of that of Adam. If the latter, then two consequences follow: (a) The subject matter is the pattern of the life of Jesus of history, which leads to exaltation (a two-stage Christology); and (b), "to be grasped" must mean *to be grasped at, snatched at, reached for*—so that equality with God is something to be gained rather than retained. On the other hand, if the former is likely, then (a) the subject matter is an event which begins and ends in heaven (a three-stage Christology), and the way of the Jesus of history is part of a downward movement, from equality with God to its opposite—obedience to the point of death; and (b), "to be grasped" must mean *retained* rather than *gained,* so that equality with God is not hung onto. Both lines of explanation have ardent supporters; on the whole, it is likely that the hymn does begin with the preexistent One who came to pass as a human being, and so on.

To be pursued here is Paul's interpretation of this christological tradition. Unfortunately, when he wrote verse 5 to stitch the tradition into his discussion, he omitted the verb! Every translation, however, must supply one, and each thereby discloses the translators' understanding of Paul, as the following samples show.

> RSV   Have this mind among yourselves which you *have* in
>   Christ Jesus.
> NEB   Let your bearing towards one another *arise* out of
>   your life in Christ Jesus.
>   *or*
>   Have that bearing towards one another which *was*
>   also *found* in Christ Jesus.

Did Paul urge readers to have a shared mind-set determined by the character of the whole event, or was that mind-set to imitate "the mind of Christ," the humble attitude of the Jesus of history? If the hymn celebrates Christ as the counterpart to Adam, then Paul's exhortation is a rather straightforward appeal to duplicate this mind-set of Jesus. But if the hymn has in view the cosmic reaches of the Christ-event, as is likely, then Paul's exhortation calls for the Christian mind-set to be formed by the character of an event which spans heaven and earth. There is no doubt that Paul interprets the hymn "ethically" (Phil 2:1-4), but it is not the ethic of the "imitation of Christ." It is rather the ethic which arises in response to an event that began before Jesus came to pass. In other words, just as Paul had interpreted Christology as the basis for justification by faith, so here he interprets the Christ-event as the basis for ethics.

We find the same interpretive move in *Second Corinthians 8:9*, where Paul provides a christological warrant for his appeal for money: "For you know the grace of our Lord Jesus Christ, that though he was rich, yet for your sakes he became poor, so that by his poverty you might become rich." Paul is not thinking of the self-impoverishment of the Nazarene carpenter who gave up a promising trade in order to become a mendicant preacher; rather, this is Paul's way of interpreting the incarnation into the human condition, understood here as "poverty" just as in Philippians 2:7 it is characterized as "slavery."

> ● Since meaning is a transaction with the text or tradition—an event rather than a thing—an interpreter should not eschew a bold restatement of what has "come home" to him or her. Interpreting the incarnation is not the same as explaining its rationale; it is, rather, expressing that rationale in another context, in another idiom.

In sum, Paul's letters show him to be not the creator of Christology, but the most penetrating interpreter of the church's emerging Christology.

Paul as Interpreter of Ethical Traditions

Paul's ethics, too, appropriates and interprets traditional material and motifs. Strictly speaking, of course, Paul neither teaches ethics nor relies on the traditions of ethics in antiquity, insofar as "ethics" has to do with critical reflection on the doer and on the good to be done. He provides no discussion of the classical virtues, nor does he compose mini-essays on such topics as friendship, honesty, and statecraft. His letters are not composed for the "religious public" in general but for specific congregations whose evolving ethos he tries to shape in accord with the gospel. Paul exhorts, counsels, urges, admonishes. To do so he draws upon a remarkable repertoire of ideas, counsels, terms, biblical passages, and insight.

The foregoing discussion has already alerted us to the Christomorphic character of Paul's moral counsel. This holds true also of the many passages in which Paul's exhortations make no explicit reference to the Christ-event, although this provides the framework, tacit or explicit, for his advice to his churches. Much the same is true also of the eschatological horizon—Paul's conviction that with Christ a new situation was inaugurated, but which is to be consummated shortly. In other words, Paul's ethics is addressed to fellow Christians who must make day-to-day decisions in light of both the "already" and the "not yet."

Sex and Marriage. In First Corinthians 7, Paul begins his response to a series of questions which the Corinthian congregation had put to him in a letter, unfortunately lost. Paul also had personal reports from "Chloe's people" (relatives, business associates? [1:11; probably also 5:1]). Moreover, the lost letter mentioned in 5:9 must have been prompted by information about the state of affairs in Corinth. In other words, whereas scholars have devoted an enormous amount of energy and inventiveness to reconstructing the situation into which Paul sent his counsel, Paul's letter could assume the situation and merely allude to aspects of it.

Paul was grappling with two opposite tendencies which developed from the same standpoint—the long-accepted Greek dualism of body and soul/spirit. This dualism evidently prompted some new Christians in Corinth to move into asceticism—a body-denying attitude based on the conviction that the material sensate body hampers the soul and so must be subdued. The same dualism evidently prompted others to conclude that the salvation of the eternal *soul* implies that the body is irrelevant; indeed, one man seems to have concluded that he would express this disdain for the body, and for the social conventions which regulated it, by cohabiting with his stepmother—a move supported by some Corinthian Christians (5:1-2). Paul, on the other hand, refused to make the body-soul/spirit dualism foundational; on the contrary, he declared roundly, "The body is for the Lord and the Lord is for the body" (6:13). Thus he interpreted the resurrection to mean that the Lord claims the body as his sphere of influence in the world. Moreover, Paul interpreted also the prevailing dualism: He agreed that the body contains the soul/spirit—not as a crate for the soul, but as the temple which houses the Spirit (6:19); therefore the Spirit's residence is to be honored. Because he asks, "Do you not know . . . ?" we may assume that he is reminding them of something that, in person, he had explained previously. The sort of thing Paul might have said is found in First Thessalonians 4:2-5, which he had written from Corinth. Here he seems to be drawing on an outline of moral instruction.

> For you know what instructions we gave you through the Lord Jesus. For this is the will of God, your sanctification: that you abstain from immorality; that each of you know how to take a wife for himself in holiness and honor, not in the passion of lust like the heathen who do not know God; that no man transgress, and defraud his brother in business, because the Lord is the avenger in all these things.

The Corinthians probably received the same instructions. Still, what does it mean to be married "in holiness and honor,

...the passion of lust"? Does this preclude sexual relations? If that is the case, then does it not follow that "it is well for a man not to touch a woman"? (1 Cor 7:1). This seems to have been the conclusion drawn by the ascetically minded in Corinth. In fact, many students conclude that this was a slogan bandied about in Corinth and that the translations should put it into quotation marks, as the Revised Standard Version does with other statements (1 Cor 6:12-13; 8:1). In any case, without now referring to the codelike instruction given at Thessalonica, Paul interprets sex and marriage as a matter of "holiness and honor." We might interpret "honor" as respect, or dignity.

Paul's opening paragraph in First Corinthians 7 makes it clear that neither the man nor the woman is to be honored on a pedestal; rather, there is mutuality because the dignity and worth of each is to be respected. It is also clear that although Paul prefers that Christians be free of involvements which distract from "undivided devotion to the Lord" (vv 35, 28-31), like Paul himself (vv 7-8), being unmarried is a gift of the Spirit not given to all. Therefore, remaining single cannot be the norm. The norm, rather, is for "each man to have his own wife and each woman her own husband" (v 2), because of the temptation to "immorality." Paul disabuses his readers of the illusion that foregoing marriage will inevitably make all Christians "more spiritual." He refuses to be lured into the position of urging a choice: Either develop your spirituality or fulfill your sexuality. For the married, his concern is for sound spirituality and healthy sexuality. Only if there is mutual consent does he sanction sexual abstinence, and then for but brief periods (v 5). The basic principle is that each belongs to the other and each owes the other "conjugal rights."

Paul's counsel is practical, down-to-earth. If he supports sexual abstinence and nonmarriage, it is not because of any sense that sex is sinful, that sexuality must be thwarted in order for one to be a first-class Christian, or that females are inherently evil or less spiritual and much more passionate. None of Paul's allegedly negative views of sex and marriage (e.g., "It is better to marry than to burn [with passion]," v 9) is based on either body-soul/spirit dualism or on female inferiority. His views are grounded not so much in nature as in time—the sense that time is running out (v 29). Why undertake the responsibilities and involvements of family life if the transformation of all things is at hand? It never occurred to Paul to draw the opposite conclusion—get married promptly while you still can, otherwise you will miss out on something. For him, sex and marriage are neither sin to be avoided at all costs nor salvation to be seized without delay. They are, instead, powerful and demanding realities of this age, to be dealt with pragmatically for the well-being of all.

Paul's freedom from ideological approaches to sex and marriage and his commitment to practical counsel manifest themselves especially in his treatment of divorce. Not only does he clearly distinguish his own judgment from the Word of the Lord (vv 8, 10, 12), but he recognizes that there may be circumstances when even the Word of the Lord might not be honored. Paul explicitly refers to the tradition of Jesus' teaching which, according to Mark 10:2-12, prohibits divorce—though Moses provided for it as a concession to the human heart. In Jesus' context, husbands could divorce wives, but not the reverse; Paul, however, formulates Jesus' teaching in a way that parallels the parity of each person having his or her own spouse (vv 10-11):

> the wife should not separate from her husband
> the husband should not divorce his wife.

(There is no difference in meaning here between "separate" and "divorce.") Into the middle of this formulation Paul inserts a parenthesis: "But if she does, let her remain single or else be reconciled with her husband." (The fact that this exception is not repeated for the man reflects Paul's sensitivity to style, not a disparity in his counsel.) Paul was not the only writer to adjust Jesus' teaching. Matthew 5:32-33 and 19:9, while reflecting the Jewish custom of male-initiated divorce, allow for an exception in the case of *porneia,* a word used for a wide range of sexual activity regarded as immoral (RSV's "unchastity" is too specific). Some students believe it refers to illicit marriages (e.g., step-sister). In any case, compared with Matthew, Paul does not specify the circumstance when an exception can be made to Jesus' teaching. He simply assumes that there will be occasional divorce. (Even if, as is sometimes held, the parenthesis is from the hand of a later scribe, it is remarkable that no basis for the exception is given.)

In verses 12-16, Paul interprets the sex and marriage tradition into a problem Jesus never had to face—mixed marriages between members of the church and non-believers. Paul interprets the prohibition against divorce as meaning that the believing spouse should not appeal to the Christian faith in order to initiate divorce if the unbelieving spouse is willing to remain married. The holiness or sanctity of the believer is not annulled by having sex with an unbelieving spouse; on the contrary, the unbeliever is made holy by the believer, and children born of such a union are holy as well. In other words, because Paul sees the possibility of "sanctification" for the unbeliever, he does not worry about the possible "contamination" of the believer. Besides, the story has not yet ended—the nonbeliever may become a believer. Paul recognizes that faith in Christ, baptism, and membership in the church can become the occasion for domestic friction; yet the believer should not use the occasion to seek divorce. Paul understands himself to be a faithful interpreter of the Jesus-tradition about divorce, even as he makes adjustments.

● Today's interpreter (of both Jesus and Paul) also needs to take into account the quite different social realities to which the same words—*marriage, divorce, betrothal*—refer.

● The interpreter should interpret what Paul says, not what he does not say. That is, one should not "interpret" Paul as having no positive views of marriage, and sex within it, as means of fulfillment. Likewise, his silence about those who prefer nonmarriage as a means of self-fulfillment should not be "interpreted," but simply acknowledged.

● Paul's concern for the sanctity of marriage as a human institution, and for the sanctity of the children whose dignity and environment deserves to be respected, merits interpretation into our own context, which differs from Paul's as much as his differs from that of Jesus.[1]

Diets and Deities (1 Cor 8, 10; Rom 14–15). Students of religion are fascinated by the diverse religious sanctions and taboos associated with food. (Most religions, after all, are a matter of practices more than of clearly formulated beliefs.) Certain foods are either prohibited (e.g., pork among Jews and Muslims) or required (e.g., mushrooms in certain groups). Moreover, in antiquity, it was common either to place some symbolic food at a shrine or to hold a cult meal there so that the deity could share in it. Furthermore, the line between slaughtering an animal and sacrificing it was a fine

[1]Specific ways in which Paul's discussion in 1 Cor 7 may be pertinent today are explored in V. P. Furnish, *The Moral Teaching of Paul: Selected Issues* (Nashville: Abingdon Press, 1979), chap 2.

one; consequently, butchers customarily sent a part of the
carcass to the shrine, just as priests sold the bulk of the
sacrifice to the meat market. Other religious traditions, then
as now, advocated vegetarianism, while some forbade even
certain vegetables (e.g., Neo-Pythagoreans did not eat
beans). Given the pluralism of Greco-Roman culture, these
diverse practices and their rationales existed side-by-side, as
they do today, and doubtless were taken with as wide a range
of seriousness as well.

The movement of Christianity into the Greco-Roman
world inevitably created conflict over such customs. In the
first place, common meals were a regular feature of the
Christian community from the beginning (e.g., Acts 2:46).
As long as everyone at the table was a Jew, matters of diet
simply did not arise. But when the congregations in the
hellenistic cities began to include Gentiles, who did not share
Jewish food customs, problems arose, made more intense by
the fact that then there was no sharp separation between the
Lord's Supper and church supper. This dilemma is reflected
in Galatians 2:11-14. Even among congregations that were
primarily Gentile, questions arose about what could and
could not be eaten. These issues could easily tear the
communities apart, because everyone had opinions about
what was acceptable. It is not surprising, therefore, that the
issue of food should appear again and again in the New
Testament, or that it is treated in diverse ways.

- At the same time one points out parallels between "then
and now," one should also make clear important differences—for example, modern vegetarianism often has no
clear religious referent at all, nor do some taboos such as the
refusal to eat dog or horse meat.

- "Tradition" includes not only transmitted formulae or
hymns, but customs and customary ways of thinking.

The Corinthians asked Paul also about "food offered to idols" (1 Cor 8:1). His response is somewhat complex, for not only does chapter 9 interrupt it, but 10:1-22 seems to have in mind a somewhat different aspect of the problem ("worship of idols," 10:14) and takes a more rigorous line in response. Accordingly, it has been proposed that in chapters 8 through 10 we have parts of different letters to Corinth placed side by side. Be that as it may, Paul's discussion exemplifies his work as an interpreter, for he weaves together theology, pastoral concern, and reflections on certain themes such as conscience and freedom. At the same time, he interprets not only Christian faith but the Corinthians' own thinking. Some years later when he wrote Romans, he rethought the matter. Thus in a sense, Paul interprets himself.

The Revised Standard Version puts into quotation marks "All of us possess knowledge" (1 Cor 8:1), just as it does "All things are lawful" in 10:23, because the translators are persuaded, rightly, that these are slogans being used in Corinth (and perhaps cited in the letter to Paul). Since First Corinthians 8:7 says "Not all possess this knowledge," probably "all of us" actually means "all of us who think this way"—in other words, a certain group, which probably also claimed, "All things are lawful." These folk were convinced that anything could be eaten because Christ had liberated them from all food taboos. It is important to note that Paul agrees with them. It is equally important to see that Paul makes it clear that some things are more important than being right: love for one's fellow Christian and "building up" the community as a whole, rather than fracturing it—" 'Knowledge' puffs up, but love builds up" (8:1).

After putting "knowledge" into perspective, Paul interprets a rudimentary aspect of knowledge of God—monotheism (1 Cor 8:4-6). In a polytheist culture, the

Christians shared with Judaism, and with certain philosophical traditions, the insistence that there is but one God;
this was part of Paul's gospel to the Greco-Roman world (1
Thess 1:9-10). Accordingly, Paul and the Corinthians agree
that "an idol has no real existence." At the same time, he
recognizes that many gods and "lords" are in fact being
worshiped. Still, for Christians there is but one God and one
Lord; the relation to the one God and one Lord is expressed,
interestingly enough, with the help of stock phrases from
popular philosophy. The group in Corinth probably
appealed to Paul's own teaching. He might have encouraged
"his side" to persist. In fact, however, he told them to back
off. Why?

Because not all members of the house church have
sufficiently assimilated monotheism; for them, "There is no
God but one" is still merely "theoretical"; they have not yet
reached the point where they really believe that the gods
they had worshiped a few months before really do not exist
and that food offered to those gods was offered to nothing.
Inwardly, they are not free to eat it. Yet if they do eat it, they
compromise their sensibilities—or as Paul puts it, "Their
conscience, being weak, is defiled." They might follow the
example of the "knowledgeable" who join friends at a meal
at the shrine, yet not be able to do so "in good conscience."
When this happens, the freedom of the knowledgeable
brings about the ruin of the scrupulous; even worse, by
asserting one's right to be right, one sins against the brother
or sister, and so sins against Christ himself. Paul concludes,
"If food is a cause of my brother's falling, I will never eat
meat, lest I cause my brother to fall" (1 Cor 8:13). Does Paul
ask the knowledgeable to forfeit their freedom? Not at all.
He asks them to exercise their freedom—the freedom to
forego manifesting their freedom, for the sake of a
fellow-believer. What Paul is proposing is the responsible

use of freedom. The believer who knows that "food will not commend us to God. We are no worse off if we do not eat and no better off if we do" (v 8), is the one who is free to eat or not to eat.

In 10:23–11:1 Paul continues the discussion, this time using as his springboard the slogan, "All things are lawful" (i.e., everything is permitted). Again he agrees, but counters, "But not all things are helpful" or "build up" the community. Whereas Philippians 2:4 counsels the readers to seek *also* the well-being of others, here Paul places the "good of the neighbor" ahead of one's own (1 Cor 10:24). Having restated his principle, Paul takes up three situations: (a) When you do the buying, ask no questions about what is sold; (b) when someone else has done the buying and the cooking, ask no questions (in either case, don't make an issue of it); (c) when someone else (presumably a scrupulous Christian) does make an issue of it, respect *that* person's conscience—don't eat. Your own conscience is not affected. This much is clear. What is not clear is the second half of verse 29 and verse 30, for Paul seems to be objecting to what he has just written. Perhaps the New English Bible has solved the problem by regarding these questions as Paul's formulation of the reader's objection: " 'What?' you say, 'is my freedom to be called in question by another man's conscience? If I partake with thankfulness, why am I blamed for eating food over which I have said grace?' " On this basis, 10:31–11:4 would be Paul's own reply.

In 10:1-22, Paul seems to interweave the issues of "food offered to idols" (10:19) and "worship of idols"; moreover, he insists that Christians cannot allow themselves to become involved, even implicitly, with the latter (v 14). In this passage there is no concern for conscience at all; rather the key word is *koinōnia* ("participation"), and the warrant for nonparticipation is sacramental. Christians are allowed only one participation—in the blood and body of Christ. Here Paul says that "food offered to idols" is offered "to demons and not to God" (v 20). The problem seems to be not what is sold in the butcher shop (a token of which had been sent to a temple), but what is offered to the deity at the shrine and consumed on the grounds by the worshipers in some sort of sacred meal. In 8:10 Paul had allowed Christians to eat a temple meal as long as a "weaker" fellow-believer had no problems, but in chapter 10 he forbids participation, because "You cannot partake of the table of the Lord and the table of demons." Either he has in view two kinds of meals, the one permissible in principle and the other not, or else he changed his views (i.e., we have different counsels from different letters). If the latter, then the more rigorous either/or approach is probably the earlier of the two, since Romans 14–15, written later, is consistent with First Corinthians 8.

Romans 14:1–15:13 is a discrete section which concludes Paul's exhortations begun at 12:1. What concerns us here is the way Paul expands his view in First Corinthians 8 into a general position; "idol meat" itself is not mentioned at all. Whereas First Corinthians 8 speaks of a person "weak in conscience," here Paul writes of the person who is "weak in faith" and, although he does not actually use "strong in faith," identifies himself with those who are "strong" (Rom 14:1; 15:1). Now he says flatly, "I know and am persuaded in the Lord Jesus that nothing is unclean in itself"; yet, in keeping with First Corinthians 8:7 (the scrupulous "eat food as really offered to an idol"), he adds that (some) food "is unclean for anyone who thinks it is unclean" (Rom 14:14; see also v 20). That is, he continues to emphasize the sensibility of the "weaker" person. Likewise, he insists again that each person should put the well-being of the neighbor first—that is, the "strong" ought to "bear with the failings of the weak," in accord with the demeanor of Christ (15:1-3). Paul does not appeal to the words of Jesus; the tradition of Mark 7:1-23 is apparently unknown to him. Paul's attitude toward clean and unclean food is 180 degrees away from that of his pre-Christian Pharisaism.

What is really new here, however, in addition to the inclusion of days and drink (Rom 14:5, 21), is Paul's defense of those "weak" persons whose scrupulous practices differ from his own. In First Corinthians 10:31 he had urged, "Whether you eat or drink, or whatever you do, do all to the glory of God." Now he says flatly that both the eater and the abstainer do so "in honor of the Lord" (Rom 14:6). Therefore the exhortation has a twofold concern: that no one be judgmental about the neighbor's practice (14:3-4) and that the strong not cause the weak to stumble (14:13, 20-23). The latter point elaborates First Corinthians 8:9-13, but is now put as a matter of faith and doubt. The person who is not fully persuaded that "nothing is unclean in itself" but who, for whatever reason (e.g., fear of being disdained), eats nonetheless "is condemned . . . because he does not eat from faith." Now comes the most radical view of sin in the whole Bible: "Whatever does not proceed from faith is sin" (Rom 14:23). Whoever is "justified by faith"—that is, whoever stands in a right relationship with God by the entrustment of the self to God as proclaimed in the gospel—*is* rightly related to God and therefore can eat or not eat, "For the kingdom of God does not mean food and drink but righteousness and peace and joy in the Holy Spirit" (14:17). In other words, since a right relationship with God by faith (or trust) is what matters, the strong person who induces the weak to eat, despite scruples, is committing a sin against the neighbor because this trust in God is being compromised; and the weak person who eats, but not in faith, is also committing a sin. Paul has moved 180 degrees—not only from his former Pharisaism, but also from every attempt to deal with such matters on the basis of rules.

Paul's freedom, and his interpretation of freedom, were too radical for Christians even in the first century. He stands almost alone in this regard. For one thing, he never mentions the so-called Apostolic Decree (Acts 15:23-29), which specified that Gentile Christians must "abstain from what has been sacrificed to idols and from blood" (some mss. add "and from what is strangled"). Paul's own silence about this regulation is one reason scholars doubt whether Acts is correct in placing Paul among the bearers of the "Decree" to Antioch. Moreover, later Christians who did eat "food offered to idols" are roundly condemned (Rev 2:14, 20). Only Mark 7 is consonant with Romans 14:14, but Matthew restricts this: It is eating with unwashed hands that does not defile (15:20).

> • The ethic of freedom is inseparable from the ethic of responsibility toward the fellow-Christian; to interpret Paul's ethic of freedom in terms of an alleged autonomous self and its fulfillment is contrary to Paul.

> • One may well wonder whether Paul's interpretation of diets, days, and drink is feasible apart from his understanding of justification by faith.

The survey of two major clusters of ethical issues—bed and board—has shown the extent to which Paul's exhortations and counsel are formulated in view of specific problems, which, in that form, are no longer part of the scene today. One can therefore say that the more specific Paul's counsel, the less directly transferrable into today's situation. Recognizing this does not diminish Paul's pertinence, but enhances it, for understanding Paul's precedent can prompt one to undertake analogous admonitions in an analogous way—that is, one can penetrate the Apostle's counsel and its warrants to the point where one can venture the same sort of interpretation of the gospel into the actualities of today's church in society. Doing so makes one a theologian-pastor with Paul, as well as an interpreter of him.

Paul as Interpreter of the Spirit

One vital feature of early Christian life was the experience of the Spirit. According to Acts, from Pentecost onward the Christian communities were endowed by the gift of the Spirit, which empowered the believers and initiated the Pauline mission to the Gentiles (Acts 2; 4:1-12, 31; 8:14-40; 10:44-48; 13:1-3). Although Paul never mentions the Pentecost event or the role of the Spirit in prompting his mission, it is clear from his earliest letter that also in his Gentile churches, the experience of the Spirit was essential and characteristic. He reminded the Thessalonian Christians, "Our gospel came to you not only in word, but also in power and in the Holy Spirit and with full conviction. . . . You received the word with much affliction, with joy inspired by the Holy Spirit" (1 Thess 1:5-6). In a series of terse exhortations he includes, "Do not quench the Spirit, do not despise prophesying" (5:19-20). Important as the experience of the Spirit was in Paul's churches, it appears that only in Corinth did it become a problem—probably because the dualistic mind-set in that congregation led people to revel in the experiences of power and to interpret them in a way that Paul regarded as dangerous. Nonetheless, in coping with the web of problems connected with the Spirit, Paul heeded his own advice to the Thessalonians—never did he try to "quench the Spirit," but he did insist that, apart from love, prophesying is the greatest manifestation of the Spirit's presence. In writing to the Corinthians, his aim is not

at all to urge them to become "more spiritually-minded," but
to interpret the spirituality they already have.

> • Today some interpreters will sense that their task is to
> articulate Paul's interpretation into their own Corinth-like
> situation; others will sense that their task is to undo the
> quenching of the Spirit that has already taken place.
> However, neither the explaining nor the interpreting of Paul
> will, by itself, renew the experience of the Spirit.

The Corinthian spirituality made the experience of the
Spirit the criterion for everything else. To be invaded by
divine power which brought capacities for tongue-speaking,
prophecy, healing, and the like is to be lifted out of the
ordinary into the heavenly world. It is to transcend the
mundane, to enjoy already the fullness of salvation,
understood as release from the world. The Corinthians seem
to have emphasized so strongly the "already" that there was
virtually no "not yet" of significance. They were already
"spiritual people" (pneumatikoi). In order to deflate their
balloon, Paul taunts them: "Already you are filled! Already
you have become rich! Without us you have become kings!"
(1 Cor 4:8). Moreover, since they valued the "gifts of the
Spirit" so highly, they began to line up behind their favorite
leaders. But Paul interprets precisely this factionalism in the
name of the Spirit as evidence that the Corinthians were not
at all spiritual persons but quite fleshly ones—as tart a
rebuke as one can hurl at people who regard themselves as
"spiritual" (3:1-4).

Paul's aim in First Corinthians 12–14 is to affirm the
importance of the Spirit in such a way that the unity of the
Corinthian house churches will be restored; in other words,
he interprets the "already" of the experience of the Spirit as
grounding the obligation to the congregation. Later he will

speak of the Spirit as the "first-fruits" and the "down payment" of salvation, rather than the harvest or full payment
(2 Cor 1:22; 5:1; Rom 8:23).

Paul undercuts any possible basis for pride in one's
Spirit-given gift (charisma, "begracement") by a triple
insistence on the common origin of diversity:

>   varieties of gifts—the same Spirit
>   varieties of service—the same Lord
>   varieties of effects—the same God.

Moreover, the gifts are given by God "for the common
good," not so that one person can say, "Look what I can do!"
Paul now becomes specific and lists the gifts:

>   speaking a word of wisdom
>   speaking a word of knowledge
>   faith
>   healing
>   miracle working
>   prophecy
>   ability to distinguish spirits
>   tongue-speaking
>   interpretation of tongues spoken.

It is the Spirit who energizes these capacities; they are gifts of
grace to be received gratefully and shared freely for the
common good. The Spirit's enablement does not homoge-
nize the community, but intensifies its diversity—for the
well-being of all (1 Cor 12:4-11).

To make this point clear, Paul reaches for an analogy—
one body with diverse organs. Everyone has been made a
member of the one body. Between the lines, one can hear
some Corinthians who, having received a less spectacular
gift, feel they are not quite acceptable; one can also hear the
recipients of the most prized gift, tongue-speaking, disdain

those whose gift is more ordinary. Against both, Paul insists that (a) if the foot or the ear says, "I am not part of the body," this does not make it so; (b) if the eye says to the hand, "I don't need you," this does not make it so. In fact, if one organ suffers, all suffer (1 Cor 12:12-26). The diversity of gifts is prized; no gift is too insignificant to be used for the good of all, and no gift is so powerful or dramatic that it makes one a member of an elite. Each person does what he or she is enabled to do.

Paul, having made his general point, now proceeds to rank the gifts (1 Cor 12:28-30). Some are more important *for the community* than others, even though all are valued and none disdained. This list, too, moves toward tongue-speaking, as did verses 8-10. There, however, one could receive the impression that tongue-speaking and its interpretation are the highest gifts; here, it stands at the bottom:

> first   apostles
> second prophets
> third   teachers
> then   miracle workers
>   healers
>   helpers
>   administrators
>   tongue-speakers.

Apostles head the list because it was to them that the risen Lord was made manifest, as Paul will remind the readers when he gets to chapter 15. Interestingly enough, we hear nothing more of healers and miracle-workers in Paul's churches; who the teachers were and what they taught also remain obscure. What we do learn more about is tongue-speaking and prophecy, evidently because these were the gifts that created problems of a special kind.

The Corinthians interpreted the ability to speak extraordinary syllables and words as evidence that, through the Spirit, they momentarily escaped the bondage of the body, history, and time where ordinary language was used. Glossolalia was being interpreted as evidence that they were truly spirit-people who already could speak the "tongues of angels." Prophecy, on the other hand, was intelligible speech, the ability to discern and express the will of the Lord.

Paul has received both gifts (1 Cor 14:18-19), but he puts prophecy ahead of tongue-speaking, though he is careful not to say anything that could appear to stifle such a gift (14:5). Tongue-speaking, he points out, benefits only the person who does it, unless someone else, also moved by the Spirit, interprets—states intelligibly what the tongue-speaker utters (14:6-12). In other words, Paul does not interpret the gifts but the situation in which the gifts are exercised. This leads him to take account of the presence of people who are guests at the meeting of the house church (14:23-25). A roomful of tongue-speakers under the sway of the Spirit will induce the guests to conclude that they are among the mad; but an assembly of prophets will, presumably, induce them to acknowledge that "God is really among you." Paul goes on to insist on order and limits in the exercise of these gifts (14:26-31). But he lets drop the most remarkable thing at the end—"The spirits of the prophets are subject to prophets" (v 32).

Here is an interpretation of prophecy quite at variance with that probably held by the Corinthians, who believed that they were simply the passive instruments of the Spirit—"The Spirit made me do it!" Even the tongue-speaker can "keep silence in church and speak to himself and to God" if there is no interpreter (1 Cor 14:28). It is even more true of the prophet, whose mind is not disengaged. In short, Paul interprets these gifts in such a way as to make the recipient responsible for the exercise of the gifts.

Since Paul is a Spirit-endowed prophet, he concludes by saying that everyone who is a prophet will recognize and acknowledge that Paul's word on the subject is nothing less than "a command of the Lord" (1 Cor 14:37). Anyone who does not accept this is not accepted by Paul as a prophet, either. Thereby Paul appeals to precisely the prophet's own authorization so as to bring some order into the chaos at Corinth.

Paul as Interpreter of Scripture

Most of Paul's readers today can appreciate his interpretation in Christology, ethics, and church life, whether or not they find it congenial to their own way of thinking. When Paul the interpreter of Scripture comes into view, however, more readers are baffled (if not infuriated) than appreciative. Paul seems to be arbitrary in the way he interprets Scripture. Even though he uses the widely accepted methods of exegesis and principles of interpretation of the time, as scholars regularly point out, the result is much the same: One wonders whether Paul is not so much an interpreter of Scripture as a raider of it, willfully appropriating a line or two for his own purposes rather than interpreting what is "there."

For reasons not known, there is a marked increase in the appeal to Scripture in the course of Paul's letter writing. The earliest letter, First Thessalonians, does not appeal at all to Scripture (though 1 Thess 5:8 uses phrases from Isa 59:7); the same is true of Philippians (the hymn in chap 2 uses language of Isa 45:23). Apart from Galatians, where the subject matter makes appeal to Scripture necessary, it is in the Corinthian letters that Paul begins to support his arguments with biblical quotations; in Romans, appeal to Scripture is fundamental to the discussion. No single letter is "typical." One finds also a wide range in the way Paul uses Scripture. He sometimes quotes the Greek version exactly, sometimes adjusts the wording, sometimes paraphrases, sometimes juxtaposes two quotations in order to draw out the implication he sees. Occasionally he cites the traditional author (e.g., Moses, David, or Isaiah), but most often he introduces a citation with "as it is written." Although Galatians 4:21-31 shows that he can use allegory, allegorical interpretation is not characteristic of Paul, as it is for Philo, his Jewish contemporary from Alexandria; nor does Paul rely on parables to interpret Scripture, as did the rabbis. Also absent is the prophecy-fulfillment scheme used by Matthew: "This happened in order that what was spoken by the prophet X might be fulfilled" (or some variant thereof). What does seem to mark Paul's use of Scripture is the citing of a text as directly applicable to the issue at hand.

It is this sovereign disregard of precisely what historical-critical study emphasizes—the meaning of a passage in its original setting—that seems to put so much distance between Paul's interpretation of Scripture and our own. It is not the actual exegetical moves that distance us, because from time to time we ourselves rely on them, including allegory. Rather it is our different relation to the text. Several facets of this deserve to be identified briefly.

To begin with, Paul's Scripture was not identical with ours, which has both a pre-Christian and a Christian section. In Paul's day, there was no New Testament; indeed, apart from his own letters, our New Testament did not even exist—although antecedent materials might have been circulating in written form (e.g., cycles of sayings of Jesus known today as Q, early forms of John). Paul seems not to know of them, in any case. For him, Scripture was the sacred literature used in the synagogues. These writings had not yet been formally

canonized—that is, officially declared to be *the* body of
definitive texts, to which nothing else could be added.
Traditionally, Palestinian-Syrian Judaism is believed to have
closed the canon at Jamnia (Jabneh), thirty years after Paul
wrote First Thessalonians; the Greek-speaking synagogues,
which used the Septuagint version, never did canonize their
corpus of texts, which also included the Apocrypha.
Authoritative though these texts were in both wings of
Judaism, they were not the "Old Testament," because there
was not yet a "New" one.

Furthermore, we who live far downstream from Paul have
a long history of regarding our twofold canon as an inspired
Book about which we have formulated doctrines, over which
we have argued, and because of which churches have been
split. In this Book some Christians have claimed to find
specially revealed information about the end of the world;
others, about its origin. Some have regarded it as the charter
not only of the Christian church, but of a Christian culture,
and hence have tried to govern society by appealing to its
laws, precedents, and principles. None of these would have
been part of Paul's relation to Scripture; Back to the Bible is
a slogan he would not have understood, because for him
Scripture was not a primordially deposited norm from which
church and society have departed. He did insist that the
synagogue did not rightly understand its own text (2 Cor
3:12-18), but from his angle, the Jews' problem was not
neglect but unenlightened zeal (Rom 10:2-3).

In the third place, it is doubtful whether Paul owned a copy
of the Scriptures. It would have been far too bulky and
probably too expensive. Nor did he have access to
concordances, lexicons, and the like. Had he wished to do
so, he might have been able to check references at the local
synagogue—if he were still on good enough terms with its
leadership. For the most part, however, he relied on his

memory and on its confirmation in the weekly lections of the synagogue service. He might also have had access to brief written collections of favorite texts, "testimonies" compiled by Christian teachers—though this is not certain. Today's interpreter has access to multiple versions of the Bible at low cost, perhaps critical editions of the text in its original languages, tools of all sorts (concordances, lexicons, word studies, dictionaries, atlases—and books like this one!). One may be unsure as to whether Paul or his modern interpreter is in the more advantageous position, but there is no doubt that their relation to Scripture is fundamentally different.

Finally, Paul's historical sense was different from ours, though it is almost impossible to delineate exactly how he viewed the past. He apparently regarded Scripture as reporting a sacred history with certain turning points: Adam—Abraham—Moses—Christ. But he cannot be expected to have had a sense of the way Israel's history and faith were related historically to antiquity, to say nothing of having had some of this history fleshed out and confirmed or disconfirmed by archeology. In no case did he regard the synagogue's Scriptures as providing "historical background" for Christianity. Instead, he read Scripture christologically—as pointing to Christ and to the gospel. Indeed, he could declare that when Scripture reported God's promise to Abraham—"In thee shall all the nations be blessed"—it (Scripture!) "preached the gospel beforehand to Abraham" (Gal 3:8). Paul does not think in terms of historical development at all. When he introduced the christological tradition in Galatians 4:4 with the phrase "When the time had fully come," he was not thinking of the optimum stage in the history of civilization (e.g., Pax Romana, Roman roads, near universality of Koine Greek), but of the time fixed in advance by God. In short, if Paul had been interested at all in the "original meaning" of the text—its meaning for the

writer and the immediate readers—he would have declared
that it referred to the gospel, faith in Christ, the shape of the
Christian life and hope. As Galatians 3:8 shows, Paul would
have believed that Scripture had "pre-dicted" these in the
strict meaning of the term: *spoken beforehand,* not *forecast;*
but it is only in light of Christ and the gospel that these things
could have been seen for what they really are. In other
words, Paul did not integrate Christ and the gospel into a
historical perspective, but correlated historical antecedents
to Christ.

These beginning reflections will orient us to Paul's
differing interpretations of Abraham in Galatians and in
Romans. In *Galatians 3,* it appears that he is countering
another interpretation of Abraham—that being advanced by
those Christian teachers who were insisting that Gentile
male believers accept circumcision if they wished to be
faithful, first-class Christians (i.e., Abraham's "children").
Although we have only Paul's side of the argument, it seems
that these teachers had pointed out that Abraham too had
been circumcised after his faith had been reckoned as
rectitude by God (his circumcision is reported in Gen 17, his
faith in Gen 15). Moreover, they may also have interpreted
circumcision along the lines of Philo, for whom it symbolized
mastery of the flesh; if so, then the Galatians might have
been persuaded to accept circumcision also as a way of
symbolizing their control of fleshly impulses, in support of
their yielding to the Spirit.

Paul sees the matter quite differently. He assumes that the
Galatians did receive the Spirit, but then asks whether they
did so in connection with their faith, or "by the works of the
law" (Gal 3:2-5). Obviously it was not because they undertook to obey the commandments of the Law, otherwise
non-Christian Jews would have received the Spirit. In
Galatians 6:17, Paul grants that "the desires of the Spirit

are against the flesh," but in the next verse he draws the conclusion from the import of his rhetorical question in 3:2—"If you are led by the Spirit you are not under the law." Indeed, according to 5:6, "In Christ Jesus neither circumcision nor uncircumcision is of any avail, but faith working through love." Circumcision (and the obligation to obey the whole Law, 5:3) is simply incompetent to deal effectively with "the desires of the flesh"; instead, they are dealt with by those who belong to Christ (v 24) and live by the Spirit, which the Galatians already have. Thus the alleged goal of circumcision has been proffered fraudulently.

The same is true of the goal of becoming a child, heir, "son" of Abraham. The "sons of Abraham" are those who, like Abraham, "believed God, and it was reckoned to him as righteousness" (Gal 3:6). To undergird this, Paul cites the original promise to Abraham and his "seed" (descendants) in Genesis 12:7. Paul notes that the word is *sperma* ("seed") not *spermata* ("seeds"), and he contends that this means there is one person through whom God keeps the promise— Christ (Gal 3:26). How, then, are the Galatians—or any Gentiles—Abraham's children, beneficiaries of the promise? By being baptized into Christ, in whom (and only in whom) all religious, socioeconomic, and sexual distinctions are of no account:

> For as many of you as were baptized into Christ have put on Christ. There is neither Jew nor Greek, there is neither slave nor free, there is neither male nor female; you are all one in Christ Jesus. And if you are Christ's, then you are Abraham's offspring, heirs according to the promise. (Gal 3:27-29)

This formulation, probably a piece of baptismal tradition, clearly overshoots the target, yet Paul cites it because it makes the point: There is nothing that the Gentiles must do

to overcome the hiatus between Jew and Gentile, because
that happened when they were incorporated into Christ.
Thus also from this angle, circumcision is irrelevant; indeed,
it is worse, for in effect, it nullifies the meaning of Christ (Gal
5:2, 4).

The Galatians were being told that since Moses came after
Abraham, and since Abraham's circumcision came after his
justification, obedience to the Law (and circumcision) must
follow faith. This represented a traditional way of reading
Scripture—namely, that of hellenized Judaism, in which the
Pentateuch was read as a paradigmatic story which spelled
out the "stages of faith," an allegorical reading of the text.
Against that, Paul makes two moves. First he declares that
whatever comes later does not cancel the original—that is,
Moses does not cancel Abraham (as noted, for Paul, Moses
cannot *complete* Abraham, but only compete with him).
Second, he reduces the status of the Law by claiming that it
was "added because of transgressions" (as a useful, perhaps
necessary concession) and that it was "ordained by angels
through an intermediary"—that is, it was not given directly
by God. The Law is not inherently "against" the way of faith;
rather, it is a transitional authority, similar to the *paidagōgos*
who has charge of a child for a set period of time (Gal
3:15–4:11). In other words, Paul does not read Scripture as a
pattern of religious practices and experiences to be followed,
but as a testimony to two structures of the God/human
relationship.

We do not know what the Galatians made of Paul's radical
interpretation of Abraham. At least some must have been
persuaded by it, or we would not have the letter. In any case,
Paul prevailed because his interpretation of Scripture was
grounded in a far more penetrating theological understanding
than that of the Galatians.

● An interpretation of Scripture is christological when the event of Christ and its significance for human life is the nonnegotiable criterion. Such an interpretation involves not only a particular way of reading specific texts but also a grasp of Scripture as a whole.

● Without theological penetration of the subject matter, interpretation becomes trivial; without interpretation, theological penetration becomes arcane.

In *Romans 4,* however, Paul does not need to displace another interpretation of Genesis; now his aim is to undergird justification by faith. There is continuity in interpretation, to be sure, but there are also new accents. The following elements in Paul's interpretation can be identified briefly.

1. The same statement, "Abraham believed God, and it was reckoned to him as righteousness," begins the exposition. Having contrasted "faith" and "works" (of the Law) in Romans 3:27, Paul asks whether Genesis 15:6 means that Abraham earned his status or received it as a gift. Genesis mentions only Abraham's faith, which Paul clearly does not regard as a "work," an achievement; rather it is sheer trust. This right relationship to God (righteousness) is what forgiveness means, as a quotation from Psalm 32 is taken to imply. Thereby Paul interprets God's forgiveness as justification.

2. To answer the question as to whether this point is valid only for Jews or also for Gentiles, Paul again appeals to the sequence of events in Genesis: Abraham was justified before he became a Jew (before he was circumcised). This must mean that his justification by faith is not "for Jews only."

3. Abraham's circumcision was a sign of the faith relationship he had received while he was still a "Gentile."

So he is the "father" of all Gentile believers; at the same time, circumcision makes him the "father" of Jews *who believe*. For both groups, it is Abraham the believer, and the believer only, who matters. It is regrettable that the Revised Standard Version renders Romans 4:12 in such a way that Paul speaks of "following the example of Abraham"; he actually writes of "following the *footsteps*"—that is, repeating Abraham's way. This is why verse 16 speaks of "sharing the faith of Abraham." That is, Paul never urges his readers to "*be like* Abraham" (the example); rather he sees in Abraham's faith the prototype of what faith inherently *is*, so that Abraham is as much a Christian believer as Christian believers are Abrahamic. This is why Abraham is "the father of us all" (v 16).

4. The structure of Abraham's trust in God is stated in phrases which not only reflect the Christian understanding of God the creator and resurrector of Jesus (v 17), but which show Abraham as the alternative to the root sin of the Gentile—not giving glory to God (see Rom 1:21 and 4:20).

5. Because it is the nature and role of faith that interest Paul, he can write that "the words 'it was reckoned to him,' were written not for his [Abraham's] sake alone but for ours also" (vv 23-24).

Because Paul is concerned with justification by faith as the way to salvation for Jew and Gentile alike, he concentrates on this theme in the Abraham texts and does not, as in Galatians, introduce the christological/sacramental solution. Since circumcision is not an issue, he can treat the Law in passing (Rom 4:13-15); besides, he will deal with it twice later (chaps 5, 7). Thus Paul's interpretations of Abraham illustrate the point made repeatedly—that interpretation never occurs in the abstract, but always into a situation which elicits a fresh look at the text—and another, perhaps more germane insight into it and from it.

V. THE PAULINE TRADITION INTERPRETED

As we have seen in chapter 3, after Paul's death the interpreter became the one interpreted. The purpose of this chapter is to examine several passages from the so-called Deutero-Pauline letters, writings which represent various attempts by the post-Pauline church to adapt, interpret, and even to supplement the Pauline tradition. Conditions in the world, in the Christian congregations, and in the daily lives of individual believers had changed considerably by the time these writings were produced in the last decades of the first and the early decades of the second century:

The Jewish revolt against Rome had been crushed.

Christianity was now largely a Gentile movement.

Separated as they were from the Jewish community, believers were now more susceptible to the pressures and more exposed to the hostility of society at large.

The broadening appeal of the gospel opened the way for greater ideological diversity and controversy within the church.

Christian people were forced to come to terms with the fact that Christ had not yet returned, despite the hopes and teachings of the first Christian generation.

The authors of the Deutero-Paulines share a common reverence for the apostolic traditions and apostolic office, as represented above all by the Apostle Paul. Moreover, their common concern is to apply the apostolic traditions and authority in a meaningful way to the practical needs of individual Christians, local congregations, and the church as a whole. It is only in this very practical sense that these writers are interested in enlarging the church's understanding of its gospel. They are not interested in the redefinition or refinement of basic insights and convictions. On the contrary, they accept as normative the earlier formulations of those and seek to interpret their implications for the daily lives of their readers.

This orientation to the Pauline tradition is strikingly apparent when one observes how little concern the Deutero-Paulinists manifest for the interpretation of Scripture (our Old Testament). At various points in his letters the Apostle himself had sought to develop or support important theological points on the basis of scriptural exegesis. There is none of that in the Deutero-Pauline letters. Scripture is specifically quoted only three times in Ephesians (4:8, quoting Ps 68:19; 5:31, quoting Gen 2:24; 6:2-3, quoting Deut 5:16 and Exod 20:12), only twice in the Pastorals (1 Tim 5:18, quoting Deut 25:4; 2 Tim 2:19, quoting Num 16:5 and Isa 26:13), and not at all by the authors of Second Thessalonians and Colossians. It is not the exegesis of Scripture, but the example of Paul's life and the authority of his teachings with which these writers are primarily concerned. To demonstrate this, and to demonstrate as well how the modern interpreter may go about understanding these ancient interpreters, we turn now to a consideration of several representative passages.

Second Thessalonians

The most important passage in Second Thessalonians is 2:1-12, which opens the main section of the letter. The body of this letter, as in Paul's own letters, follows a salutation (1:1-2) and thanksgiving (1:3-12) and extends through 3:13. The letter closing consists of a final warning (vv 14-15), an attestation of Pauline authorship (v 17), and two benedictions (vv 16, 18).

> ● Locating a passage within its literary context is an essential
> step as one begins one's exegesis.

The subject matter of 2:1-12 is clearly announced in the first sentence: "Now concerning the coming of our Lord Jesus Christ and our assembling to meet him . . . " (2:1). One thinks immediately of First Thessalonians 4:13–5:11, in which Christ's return and the gathering-up of believers are also discussed (see esp. 4:15-17). Here, as in First Thessalonians, the readers are given instruction on the topic; but this writer, unlike Paul in the earlier letter, is opposing a false view propagated by certain persons who have "refused to love the truth" (2 Thess 2:10; cf. vv 2-3, 11).

> ● Another important early step in interpretation is to identify
> the topic of the passage. In the present case, by doing so one
> also begins to discern something about the occasion and
> purpose of the whole letter.

This topic dominates the central section of Second Thessalonians, although the form of the discussion changes slightly in 2:13. In our passage, the form is essentially didactic,

but from 2:13 through 3:13 it is much more directly hortatory, the consequences of the teaching being spelled out for
the readers. They are to "hold to the traditions" (2:15) and
pray for the Apostle from whom they received them (3:1-2);
they are to remain obedient to his commands (3:3-5); and
they are not to be idle or condone idleness (3:6-13).

> ● Alternatively, one might divide the letter body between
> 2:17 and 3:1, corresponding to the chapter division (which is
> itself of only medieval origin), since the benediction of
> 2:16-17 certainly concludes a pericope, and the hortatory
> address "brethren" in 3:1 clearly opens a new one. The
> division between 2:12 and 2:13 is more important, however,
> and is also marked by the writer's use of a hortatory address,
> "brethren beloved by the Lord" (2:13). This second major
> division of the letter body calls the readers to consider how
> they should respond to the teaching of 2:1-12. Now the whole
> letter has been surveyed, and the interpreter is prepared to
> look more closely at the contents and function of the passage
> selected for special analysis.

This writer is opposing the notion "that the day of the Lord
has come" (v 2). How could anyone have supposed that?
Some interpreters (and also, e.g., the King James and
American Standard versions) think the claim was that the
day was "at hand," and one can more easily understand how
that view could be held. Other interpreters, however,
believe the author is confronting opponents who have
redefined the traditional eschatological hope, under the
influence of Gnostic ideas, by spiritualizing the idea of
Christ's return and his gathering-up of believers to heaven.

> ● The consulting of various translations will often alert one to
> issues of interpretation. If possible, the interpreter should
> also consult several different commentaries. When only one

is used, it should indicate the various possible ways major questions about the passage can be answered.

Whatever the case, this teaching had the effect of unsettling those who espoused it (2:1). Like some modern millennialist sects, certain believers may have been prompted by this false teaching to abandon their daily responsibilities in order to await the Lord's coming or to devote themselves to the "higher" spiritual life into which they thought they had already been gathered.

Our author's response to this false view of the Lord's return comes first of all in 2:3-4 and is supported by the comment in verse 5 that the true view is part of the tradition the readers had received from their Apostle. They are assured now that the day of the Lord will not dawn until after "the man of lawlessness . . . the son of perdition," has mounted his rebellion against God and the true worship of God. Is the author thinking of some specific historic personage, perhaps the ruling emperor in Rome or one of his representatives who poses a present threat to the church? Or is the writer simply drawing from the traditions of Jewish apocalyptic, which regularly identified the opponents of God's people with some specific blasphemy committed in or against the Temple by a political overlord? It really doesn't matter, because the author's point is that this "rebellion" has not yet occurred, so the day of the Lord must be still some time off.

The remainder of the passage, 2:6-12, elaborates and supports this argument but adds nothing substantial to it.

● With this observation one is ready to make a tentative judgment about the interior structure of the passage being examined and about the course of the argument within it: In 2:1-2, a false teaching is identified and the readers are warned

not to be taken in by it; 2:3-4, the fallacy of the teaching is
exposed; 2:5, Paul's authority is invoked; 2:6-12, the
argument is elaborated and supported, concluding with a
threat against those who allow themselves to be deceived by
the false teaching (vv 10-12).

The essential point has already been made. Since those
things which must precede Christ's return have not yet
occurred (if "the mystery of lawlessness is already at work,"
it is nonetheless still being restrained, vv 6-7), it is wrong to
say that the day of the Lord has already come (or is at hand).

Those who believe that Paul himself wrote Second
Thessalonians must explain the striking difference between
the teaching of this passage and that of First Thessalonians
4:13–5:11. In the earlier letter the Apostle had specifically
insisted that Christ's return would be like the coming of "a
thief in the night," suddenly and without warning (1 Thess
5:2-3). Here in Second Thessalonians, however, readers are
told that Christ's return will be preceded by unmistakable
events of lawlessness, by Satan's own coming "with all power
and with pretended signs and wonders" (2 Thess 2:9). It is
not impossible that Paul himself is correcting misinterpretations of his eschatological teaching by adding points he had
left out of First Thessalonians. To many, however, the
contrast in viewpoint between First and Second Thessalonians is best explained by the hypothesis that Second
Thessalonians is Deutero-Pauline. Will the Lord's return
be heralded by obvious signs—wickedness and rebellion
(2 Thess)—or will it occur without warning, when all seems
tranquil and secure (1 Thess)? The addition in Second
Thessalonians amounts to a major shift in point of view. In
First Thessalonians Paul had presumed that he himself
would still be alive at the Lord's return (see 4:17, "We who
are alive, who are left") and had urged his readers to be

constantly on the lookout for it. In Second Thessalonians, a later writer finds it necessary to reckon with an indefinite delay in the Lord's return and cautions readers that a number of major events must occur before then.

If there is any message here for present-day Christians, they will probably not find it in the admittedly obscure apocalyptic ideology of Second Thessalonians 2:1-12. However, when the teaching of this passage is read in the light of the whole letter and with reference to the situation this writer is addressing, then an important point emerges.

> • Observe in the passages that follow how the interpreter's attention to the literary context and to the sociohistorical situation which occasioned the letter enables the text itself to be appropriated.

The apocalyptic scenario of 2:1-12 is really only preliminary to the practical appeals of 2:13–3:13, in particular those of 3:6-13. The author wants the readers to understand that as long as this world endures, the Christian's place is within it, fully engaged with everyday responsibilites. Apocalyptic fanatics, who by giving up those responsibilities have become dependent on other members of the Christian community, are no longer to be supported.

> • This, in context, is the meaning of Second Thessalonians 3:10*b*, "If any will not work, let him not eat." It is perverse to use this and related texts (3:6, 8, 11, 12) as sanctions against public welfare programs or private charities for those who, by reason of circumstance, are unable to support themselves.

While the ideology of Second Thessalonians 2:1-12 is unparalleled in Paul's own letters and difficult to reconcile with the apocalyptic scenarios in First Thessalonians 4–5 and

First Corinthians 15, the call to Christians to be responsible members of their community is thoroughly Pauline. Indeed, in Second Thessalonians, this later writer has applied the Apostle's own more general appeals in First Thessalonians 2:9-12 and 5:12-22 to the specific problem of disengagement from everyday life which he sees occurring in certain Christian circles. Like the Apostle whose authority he invokes, the author of Second Thessalonians believes that the Christian's hope should undergird, not undermine the Christian's commitment to a life of responsible service in the world. In this respect, at least, he is an authentic interpreter of the Pauline tradition.

Colossians

The author of this letter, like the other Deutero-Pauline writers, follows closely the formal pattern of the genuinely Pauline letters. The letter opening includes a salutation (1:1-2) and a thanksgiving (1:3-8), and the closing consists of commendations (4:7-9), greetings (4:10-15), special instructions (4:16-17), and an apostolic attestation and benediction (4:18). The body of the letter, which runs from 1:9–4:6, focuses above all on the lordship of Christ. An affirmation of his preeminence (1:9–2:7) is followed by a warning about false teachers who would deny it (2:8-23), and this is followed in turn by a series of exhortations to believers to lead their lives in accord with what Christ has accomplished for them (3:1–4:6).

While it is clear enough that Colossians was written to oppose an errant "philosophy" which, in this writer's view, seriously compromised the Pauline understanding of the redemptive work of Christ, commentators differ in their views of exactly what kind of teaching is being rejected here. What can be known of it must be derived mainly from Colossians 2:8-23. That passage, more than any other, provides the interpreter with the occasion and purpose of the letter. Whether this writer thought of the teaching being opposed as a specifically "Colossian heresy" cannot be determined. (Colossae, which had been destroyed by an earthquake shortly before Paul's death, was evidently not a very important place when this letter was written.) But it is clear that the writer regarded the teaching as a threat to the faith of those Christians, whoever they were, for whom this letter was intended. The examination of two passages from two different sections of the letter body will enable us to see how the Pauline tradition is invoked to combat the threat.

Colossians 1:15-20. This pericope stands in the first main section of the letter body (1:9–2:7) and is the heart of the affirmation made there about the preeminence of Christ. The affirmation, however, is at the same time an appeal, as the hortatory conclusion to the whole section shows: "As therefore you received Christ Jesus the Lord, so live in him . . . " (2:6-7). The author's fundamentally hortatory intentions are also evident in the opening intercessions to God, asking that the readers be enabled "to lead a life worthy of the Lord, fully pleasing to him" (1:10).

The more immediate literary context of our passage is supplied by the affirmations of God (1:13) and Christ (1:14) which precede and introduce it, and by the affirmation of the readers which follows it (1:21-23).

> • Interpreters who are able to consult the Greek text of Colossians will observe just how closely 1:15-20 is connected to what has preceded. In Greek, verse 15 begins with the relative pronoun "who," referring to "his beloved Son" (Christ) in verse 13, just as verse 13 itself opens with the same relative pronoun, referring to "the Father" in verse 12. Thus the intercessory words of 1:9-12 lead directly to the affirmations in verses 13-14, and verses 15-20 continue those.

Although verses 21-23, too, constitute an affirmation, it is primarily addressed to those for whom this letter is intended (note "and you . . ." [v 21], and "provided that you . . ." [v 23]).

Specifically, verses 15-20 enlarge the affirmation of Christ begun in 14. The focus shifts, however, setting verses 15-20 apart, because Christ's saving work for believers, which is the subject of the affirmation in verse 14, is scarcely mentioned in the affirmation of 15-20 (only in v 20, and there almost incidentally). The affirmation in these verses is concerned almost exclusively with the cosmic role and status of Christ.

● Most lectionaries include this passage among their selections from Colossians, but it is usual to begin the pericope with Colossians 1:12, perhaps under the influence of the King James Version. Our analysis of the context suggests, however, that a lection might more properly begin with verses 13-14 and that, even then, the interpreter must be alert to the distinctiveness of the affirmation in verses 15-20.

On the basis of its formal structure alone, our passage is readily divisible into two main sections: verses 15-18*a* and verses 18*b*-20. The opening words of each section are (in Greek) "Who is," translated "He is" in the Revised Standard Version. (The words "he is" in RSV vv 17 and 18*a* translate a different Greek phrase.) There are, in addition, several other parallels between the two divisions: In verse 15 and again in 18*b*, Christ is called "the first-born"; the phrase "in heaven and on earth" in 16 is echoed in 20, "whether on earth or in heaven"; there are references in both divisions to the unity of "all things" in Christ (vv 16, 17; v 20; cf. v 18*b*); and the phrases "in him," "through him," and "to him" in verse 16 (RSV translates "for him") are picked up again in the same order in verses 19-20 (where RSV translates "to himself"). A number of commentators believe that these features, as well as the distinctive theme and terminology of the passage, mark it as a hymn, and The Jerusalem Bible prints it as such, divided into two main strophes as suggested by the parallelism we have observed.

> • The paraphrasing, the punctuation (including the use of quotation marks), and the identification of a text as prose or poetry, which one finds in modern versions of the Bible, have all been determined by translators and editors, not by the original authors. This is another reason interpreters should avail themselves of various translations, since judgments about such matters often vary from one to another.

We have already seen that Paul himself occasionally incorporated hymnic texts into his letters (note the discussion of Phil 2:6-11, pp. 78-81), and the author of Colossians may well have done the same thing here. If so, two important consequences follow for the interpreter. First, some attempt should be made to understand what the hymn represents in and of itself, quite apart from the letter in which it now stands. This will involve some consideration of its possible origin and original function. Second, the interpreter will want to determine the purpose the cited material seems intended to serve in its present literary context, and whether it has been adapted or altered in order to serve that purpose.

> • For help in considering these questions, most interpreters will be dependent on the specialized knowledge and expertise of biblical scholars, to which the better commentaries will provide access.

On these matters, as on the question of whether a hymn has been used here at all, the experts disagree. That is no reason for an interpreter to dismiss the matter as irrelevant, however. At the least, one needs to be aware of the issues and of the decisions any given commentator has made about them. Otherwise, one's exposition of the passage may end by being a confused amalgam of insights drawn from commentators who have made very different decisions about the various contexts within which the passage has a meaningful place.

There is widespread agreement that, whether or not these verses have a hymnic origin, the terms in which they affirm the universal lordship of Christ have been influenced by their use among hellenistic Jews. Thus the first-century Jewish philosopher Philo of Alexandria described the Logos, God's Word, as "himself the image of God . . . placed nearest, with no intervening distance, to the Alone truly existent One"; and in the Wisdom of Solomon 7:25-26, God's Wisdom is called "an image of his goodness." These passages suggest that when Christ is called "the image of the invisible God" in Colossians 1:15, it is the intimacy of the relationship between the Son and the Father that is primarily in view. Philo also refers to the Logos as "the first-born," by which he does not mean that the Logos was created first, but that the Logos was one of a kind and was, in fact, preexistent with God. The same is said of Wisdom (Prov 8:22; Sir 1:4, 24:9), just as it is said of Christ in Colossians 1:15, 18*b*, in which his role as the agent and norm of creation is being stressed (vv 16, 17). Again, just as Philo wrote of the Logos as having the same place in the cosmos as "the head does in the body regarded as a unity," so Christ is called "the head of the body, the church" (Col 1:18*a*), and the unity of that Body under Christ's headship is emphasized (v 20).

● These notes about specific terms and concepts in Colossians 1:15-20 are only exemplary of the insights a thorough analysis of the passage will yield. The fact that the christological images used here were familiar in the non-Christian world does not detract from their significance as applied to Christ. To the contrary, it shows that the church desired to affirm Christ's sovereignty by assigning him titles that were both impressive and familiar. Another of these images is the concept of "the fulness of God," used in verse 19 and again in 2:9. The more one is able to learn about the background of such christological images, the better one's understanding of the concepts they were meant to convey.

In the first part of this passage (the first strophe of the hymn) Christ is affirmed as the preexistent One who, as such, serves as the agent of creation (v 16). In the second part he is affirmed as the agent of the new creation by reason of his resurrection from the dead (vv 18*b*, 20). Running throughout is an emphasis on his universal lordship (e.g., v 15, "all creation"; v 18*b*, "in everything") and the consequent unity of all things in him (vv 17, 20). While it is the cosmic scope of Christ's work that is stressed, the historical dimensions of that work are also present, although less prominently, in references to the church (v 18*a*) and the cross (v 20)—both sometimes identified as interpolations into a hymn that, in itself, lacked any historical references.

> ● Here the content of the passage is analyzed without reference to its context. This is an especially important step if one is inclined to the possibility that these lines once existed apart from this letter, as a hymn.

What function does this affirmation of Christ's universal lordship serve within its immediate literary context (Col 1:9–2:7) and in this letter as a whole? It is clearly intended to support first the kinds of general appeals one finds in 1:10—to walk worthily of the Lord; and in 2:6-7—to live in him. These first paragraphs of the letter are calling the readers to remain faithful to the Pauline traditions (1:23), though the Apostle himself is "absent in body" (2:5). Beyond this, however, and more specifically, the affirmation in 1:15-20 provides a kind of kerygmatic foundation for the warning in 2:8-23 about certain false teachers who do not hold fast to Christ as the head of the Body (2:16-19).

Various particular elements in Colossians 1:15-20 are present also in Paul's own letters. There, too, Christ is called "the image of God" (2 Cor 4:4; cf. 3:18), and in Romans 8:29, as here in Colossians, the concepts of "image" and being "first-born" are combined with reference to Christ. Paul, too, refers on occasion to cosmic "principalities and powers" over which Christ is sovereign (Rom 8:38; 1 Cor 5:24); he, too, employs the concept of "reconciliation" to refer to Christ's saving work (Rom 5:6-11; 2 Cor 5:17-20); and he, too, can think of the church as Christ's "body" (1 Cor 12:12-30; Rom 12:4-8). But the image of Christ as the "head" of the body which we meet here in Colossians (and in Ephesians) is not present in the Apostle's own letters. In fact, it is incompatible with the underlying concept in First Corinthians 12, where Christ is identified with *all* the members of the body—there the "head" has no special place (see 12:21). Moreover, Paul himself thinks of Christ's lordship and reconciling work primarily in historical, not in cosmic terms—for example, in Romans 8:31-39, it is the sovereignty of Christ's love "for us" that is affirmed (vv 32, 35, 37, 39); and in Romans 5 and Second Corinthians 5, it is God's reconciliation of "us" that is stressed.

● The interpreter must therefore avoid harmonizing the theological images and concepts of Colossians with those of the unquestionably Pauline letters. Even those who accept Pauline authorship of Colossians must acknowledge a shift in emphasis, at least.

The "cosmic Christology" one finds here in Colossians is part of this writer's response to the teaching opposed, which, in the writer's view, seriously compromises Paul's own preaching of Christ and undermines the one true basis for the Christian life. While to the modern interpreter of Colossians it may seem that Paul's thought about Christ has been extended beyond the Apostle's own intentions, to the author of Colossians it must have seemed only that the Pauline tradition was being reaffirmed and renewed.

Colossians 3:1-17. These verses stand at the beginning of the exhortations to lead a Christian life (3:1–4:6) which constitute the last major section of Colossians. This section itself may be subdivided into smaller units. These, in turn, urge the readers to seek the things that are above (3:1-4), to put to death that which is earthly and put on that which is of God (3:5-17), to support one another in the household (3:18–4:1), to be steadfast in prayer (4:2-4), and to conduct themselves wisely toward outsiders (4:5-6). The passage before us, therefore, consists of two distinct subsections: 3:1-4 and 3:5-17.

> • Note again how interpretation begins with observations about the context and internal structure of the passage. There are, of course, various ways to define and describe these, so one must remain open to other possibilities as analysis of the passage proceeds.

The first four verses provide a transition from the earlier chapters of this letter to the exhortations that follow. In particular, this opening paragraph builds on the affirmation of Colossians 2:11-15 that baptism means burial and resurrection with Christ (2:12); or, in specifically ethical terms, appropriating God's forgiveness, which was bestowed with Christ's death upon the cross, and receiving new

life (2:13-15). That "indicative" now leads on, in good
Pauline fashion, to the "imperative" in 3:1-4. Since one has
been "raised with Christ," one should "seek the things" that
are appropriate to this new life.

We are reminded here of Paul's own discussion of the
Christian life in Romans, chapter 6. There the Apostle
himself had emphasized (a) the "newness of life" which
comes as one's old self is "crucified," then "buried" with
Christ in baptism (6:3-10); and (b) the moral obligations
thereby placed upon the believer (6:11-23). Paul, however,
had regarded the believer's resurrection with Christ as
something still to come (Rom 6:5, 8; also 2 Cor 4:14, etc.),
whereas the author of Colossians thinks of that resurrection
as having already occurred (note Col 2:12, "You *were* also
raised with him"; 2:13, "*made* alive together with him"; 3:1,
"*have been* raised with Christ"), as does the author of
Ephesians (e.g., Eph 2:1). Here in Colossians, as elsewhere
in the Deutero-Pauline materials, we see a certain "defu-
turizing" of the older Pauline eschatological hope.

That hope is still formally present, but just barely. The
only expression of it in this letter is found in 3:4. Primarily,
this author understands the believer's resurrection with
Christ as something given in and with faith itself ("You were
. . . raised with him through faith in the working of God,"
2:12). It is thus "hidden" (3:3), in the sense that it has
occurred apart from the apocalyptic events with which Paul
had specifically associated it (1 Thess 4:16-17; 1 Cor
15:20-28). This writer's method is not to reject or even
specifically to revise Paul's teaching, however, but rather to
interpret what he perceives to be its real meaning. Clearly, he
does not regard the Pauline tradition as something inert, to
be boxed up and saved in the church's theological attic like a
family heirloom. He receives it rather as a living tradition,
which grows and develops as it is interpreted and applied.

This author's Deutero-Pauline view of baptism and of the believer's resurrection with Christ is also fundamental to the more specific appeals that begin in 3:5-17. In verses 5-11 these concern mainly what the believer is to reject ("Put to death . . . what is earthly in you," v 5), whereas in verses 12-17 they concern exclusively what one is to embrace ("Put on then, as God's chosen ones, holy and beloved . . . ," v 12). These two paragraphs are best taken together, however, for "putting off the old nature" and "putting on the new nature" are clearly regarded as two sides of the same coin (vv 9-10). The vices listed in verses 5 and 8 are among those traditionally condemned by ancient authors (and not only by biblical writers), and as elsewhere, the lists are intended to be exemplary, not exhaustive.

> ● The commentaries will help the interpreter locate various biblical and nonbiblical parallels to these lists. What is most important to recognize is that they seldom reflect an author's specific knowledge about the failings of those who are being addressed.

Of special interest here is the author's conviction that the Christian's "new nature" is something that is itself "being renewed in knowledge after the image of its creator" (3:10), a striking concept which the later author of Ephesians either does not quite grasp or is unwilling to retain. (In Eph 4:23-24, renewal is understood to precede, or else to be simultaneous with putting on the new nature.)

> ● Interpreters who believe that the author of Ephesians has used Colossians will often find such comparisons illuminating. This one, for example, helps to bring out the distinctiveness of the idea of renewal in Colossians 3:10.

The statement in Colossians 3:11, that there is neither Greek nor Jew, and so on, in Christ, should be compared with similar statements in Galatians 3:28 and First Corinthians 12:13. It is probable that a baptismal formula underlies all three, but the interpreter will need to be alert to the way that formula has been variously altered to fit the specific concerns of these three specific letters. What is said here of Christ—that he is "all, and in all"—conforms to this author's emphasis on the cosmic lordship of Christ (cf. esp. 1:15-20). Paul had said the same of God in First Corinthians 15:20 ("and thus God will be all in all"; the RSV obscures the almost identical Greek wording).

Our author's positive appeals in 3:12-17 sound about as Pauline as anything in the whole letter, especially the call upon the readers to let "love" and "the peace of Christ" rule in the community of faith (vv 14-15; cf., e.g., 1 Cor, chaps 12–14). The exhortation to offer one's whole life in word and deed as an act of thanksgiving to God (v 17) is also thoroughly Pauline (note the Apostle's conception of Christian obedience as one's "spiritual worship," Rom 12:1-2), and may be compared especially with First Corinthians 10:31.

> • In cases like this, in which a Deutero-Pauline writer does little more than re-state Pauline teaching, the interpreter is justified in quoting the later text along with the earlier to help explain and support the earlier.

Ephesians

As observed in chapter 3, this so-called Letter to the Ephesians is not really a letter, though it follows to some extent the Pauline model, and it probably was not written only for the Christians of Ephesus. Moreover, its author, who seems not to have been Paul, has drawn heavily on the ideas and, in some cases, even the wording of Colossians. One's first inclination when confronted with these findings (which are accepted by many, though not by all scholarly investigators) might be to avoid Ephesians as a lost cause. That would be a mistake, however. The fact that its author knew and used Colossians (and probably other, unquestionably genuine Pauline letters) affords us a rare opportunity to discover how one early Christian writer sought to employ the Pauline tradition, as it had been received and understood, in the service of a theme the writer considered vitally important for the church of that day. That theme is the unity of the church; and the object of the author's work, which can be characterized as a laudatory discourse, is to describe and praise that unity in order that the readers might better serve it.

Chapter 1 is essentially introductory. After the salutation, which gives Ephesians the superficial appearance of a letter (1:1-2), there is a lengthy blessing which seems to draw heavily on the church's liturgical and hymnic traditions (1:3-14). Then comes the paragraph of thanksgiving that would normally follow directly after the salutation (1:15-23). The discourse proper, extending from 2:1 through 6:20, has two main parts. In the first, 2:1–3:21, the theme of the church's unity is introduced and developed with reference to the believers' resurrection with Christ (2:1-10), their reconciliation in him (2:11-22), and Paul's ministry of unity (3:1-21). In the second part, 4:1–6:20, the readers are admonished to lead a life worthy of their calling, maintaining "the unity of the Spirit in the bond of peace" (see esp. 4:1-3).

Dependence on Colossians is evident in both main sections of the discourse. The author is dependent, first of all and fundamentally, on the "cosmic Christology" of the earlier letter. Here in Ephesians that Christology has been used to support the idea of the unity of the church, a unity now understood to be based on the primordial cosmic oneness assured in God's plan for salvation. (See esp. 1:3-10, 3:11, and note the emphasis on Christ's cosmic lordship in 1:19-23.) Just as the earlier author had written of Christ as filled with God's "fulness" (Col 1:19, 2:9), so now the author of Ephesians, developing the idea of Christ as head of the Body, also met first in Colossians, writes of the church itself as God's fullness ("the fulness of him who fills all in all," Eph 1:23).

The author of Ephesians is dependent on Colossians also in various specific ways (the better commentaries provide details), and some of these can be pointed out as we examine two representative passages.

• Consultation of the parallel passage(s) in Colossians should be a routine part of one's study of Ephesians. It will often alert the interpreter to special interests and concerns of the later writer: What has been changed? What has been omitted? What has been added?

Ephesians 2:11-22. In approaching this passage the interpreter may be tempted to fasten too quickly on the well-known and often-expounded statement of verse 14 that Christ "is our peace, who has made us both one, and has broken down the dividing wall of hostility." This is without question one of the central affirmations of the passage, but it must be read in its full context. Unfortunately, ecclesiastical lectionaries, which regularly include this passage in the cycle of readings for the church, have helped to obscure that context by traditionally omitting the first two verses of the paragraph, beginning the reading only with verse 13. This has led many interpreters to neglect the fact that the subject here is, first of all, the relation of Gentile Christians to the promises bestowed upon Israel. In the context, the "dividing wall of hostility" has, initially, this very specific reference. The readers, whom the author presumes to be Gentiles, are reminded that they were at one time "separated," not only from Christ but also from "the commonwealth of Israel," from the promises on which it was founded, and therefore from God (v 12). "But now," the writer emphasizes, they have been "brought near" by the saving death of Christ, which has abolished "the law of commandments and ordinances" which heretofore had barred Gentiles from belonging to God's covenant people (vv 13-15; see also 3:6). The same basic concept, but without specific references to the Gentiles and Israel, is present in Romans 8:1-4.

It is also important to observe that this author understands the reconciliation of Jew and Gentile in Christ as part of the reconciliation of all humanity to God ("one new man in place of the two," v 15).

- The word "man," used in most translations of Ephesians 2:15, renders the Greek word *anthrōpos,* which does not in itself refer to maleness. In such cases the interpreter may quite legitimately substitute some term like *person,* or, in this instance, even *humanity.*

Moreover, our writer emphasizes that this "access . . . to the Father" (v 18) is "in one body" and "in one Spirit" (vv 16 and 18 respectively). This is in accord with the theme of Ephesians as a whole—the unity of the church ("one body and one Spirit . . . one hope . . . one lord, one faith, one baptism, one God and Father of us all," 4:4-6) and the church's role in salvation (e.g., 3:10). God's "plan for the fulness of time" involves the uniting of "all things in [Christ]" (1:10), as "all things" become subject to the resurrected Lord, exalted as cosmic Sovereign (1:20-23).

• The discussion in Ephesians is so carefully and sharply
focused on this one theme that it is not only important but
also fairly easy for the interpreter to relate the thoughts of
one passage to those of another. This should not be done
uncritically, however, but always with attention to the
context and function of each passage.

This is one of the many passages in Ephesians which seems
to have been composed by rather close reliance on
Colossians. A comparison with Colossians, 1:20, 21-23
specifically, will bring the interpreter into touch with some
further important aspects of Ephesians 2:11-22.

It may be noted first that the conception of Christ as "our
peace" in Ephesians 2:14-16 seems to have been derived
from the image of Christ as peacemaker present in
Colossians 1:20. This conclusion is supported by the fact that
Christ's role as reconciler and the cross as the means of
reconciliation, both mentioned in that same verse in
Colossians, are also prominent ideas in our passage
("reconcile us . . . through the cross," Eph 2:16; see also
Eph 2:13, "the blood of Christ"). Here in Ephesians, of
course, these ideas have been applied more specifically to
the author's concept of the integration of the Gentiles into
the destiny of God's covenant people. That is a matter about
which Colossians is silent.

A comparison of Ephesians 2:14-16 with Colossians 1:20
also accentuates the later writer's interest in the church as a
vital part of the plan of salvation. To the identification of the
cross as the means of reconciliation (Col 1:20), is now added
a reference to the church as the place of reconciliation ("in
one body through the cross," Eph 2:16). That this ecclesio-
logical dimension really does go beyond anything to be found
in Colossians is shown by Colossians 1:22 where, despite the

similar context, "body" refers to Jesus' "body of flesh," which at his crucifixion brought reconciliation.

The opening verses of our passage (Eph 2:11-12) can be profitably compared with Colossians 1:21, in which that author had addressed the readers (also presumed to be Gentile Christians) as people "who once were estranged and hostile in mind, doing evil deeds." In that context, "estranged" meant separated from God. As we have seen, however, here in Ephesians there is a special concern for the alienation of the Gentiles from the people of Israel, and thus from "the covenants of promise" (v 12). The short relative clause in Colossians 1:21 now has become, in Ephesians 2:11-12, a much longer, freestanding appeal to "remember" what that estrangement had involved.

In Colossians 1:21-23, the main point had come in verse 22, an affirmation that "in his body of flesh by his death," Christ had reconciled the readers to God. This is restated in Ephesians 2:13, but with two significant omissions. First, the reference to Jesus' crucified body is not picked up, since this writer will speak of "the one body" in another sense in verse 16. Second, this writer does not specify to what or to whom the readers have been "brought near" by Christ's death. That specification comes in verses 14-16 where, as we have seen, the reconciliation with God, the topic in Colossians 1:22, is discussed only in connection with the "one new humanity" in the "one body."

Finally, the appeal in Colossians 1:23 to "continue in the faith" (stated as a condition for one's appropriation of Christ's reconciling work) is substantially extended in Ephesians 2:17-22. The preaching of "the gospel . . . to every creature under heaven" is now identified with Christ's own preaching of "peace" to those who were "far off" (the Gentiles) as well as to those who were "near" (the Jews; Eph 2:17).

● The preaching of peace to those afar and to those who are near is also a theme in Isaiah 57:19, to which our author is probably alluding (see also Isa 52:7). The commentaries will help the interpreter identify such allusions, not all of which are as clear as this one. One should remember, however, that the determinative context for the interpretation of Ephesians 2:17 remains Ephesians 2:11-22, not Isaiah 57.

Now, too, is added a reference to the "one Spirit" in whom "both [Gentiles and Jews] have access . . . to the Father" (Eph 2:18), and two separate metaphors are invoked to describe the Gentiles' adoption into the covenant community: They have become "fellow citizens with the saints and members of the household of God" (cf. Phil 3:20; Gal 6:10, etc.). The second of these leads on to the more elaborate and quite remarkable metaphor of verses 20-23. Here believers are likened to the walls of a building founded upon the teaching of "the apostles and prophets," with "Christ Jesus himself being the cornerstone" (v 20).

There is in Colossians, of course, no parallel to verses 20-23. In verse 20 the author of Ephesians seems to be dependent upon First Corinthians 3:10-15, in which Paul himself had likened the church to a building. The church's one and only "foundation," Paul had insisted, is Jesus Christ as presented in the apostolic preaching (1 Cor 3:10-11). In Ephesians, however, we have an author who is looking *back* to Paul, concerned that the readers adhere to the apostolic norms for their Christian faith and life. Here, then, "the apostles and [Christian] prophets" themselves are identified as the church's foundation. This requires, of course, an extension of the original Pauline metaphor, since the author must still indicate the overriding importance of Christ in the church. That is why Christ is now called "the cornerstone," that stone to which all the walls of a building must be oriented if they are to be firm and true.

This metaphor is further extended in Ephesians 2:21-22. Now the building is identified as God's "temple" (see 1 Cor 3:16; cf. 1 Cor 6:19). Moreover, the inert building materials of Paul's metaphor (1 Cor 3:12) have been left behind. In this context it is *believers* (specifically, Gentile Christians) who constitute the "walls" of the church (note "You are . . . built" in Eph 2:19-20, 22), so we are invited to think of this "whole structure" as *growing* into its function as "a dwelling place of God in the Spirit." This view of the church as a vital, growing organism is rather more naturally, although perhaps not more effectively conveyed in Ephesians 4:15-16, where the church is portrayed as a body united in and ruled by Christ, its head.

● The foregoing observations about Ephesians 2:11-22 are intended to illustrate just two things, but both are important. First, when one is confronted with a text as familiar and as frequently expounded as Ephesians 2:14, one has a special responsibility to understand its function and meaning in the passage of which it is a part. We have seen that the topic here is rather specifically the integration of the Gentiles into "the commonwealth of Israel," defined not as a community of those bound to God through their obedience to the Law, but as a commonwealth where "citizenship" is given through the reconciling work of Christ the peacemaker. The reference in verse 14 to "the dividing wall of hostility" is not to the various social barriers which crisscross society at large, including the church, as a result of bigotry and prejudice. It refers to the *theological barrier* of the Law, by which the Gentiles had been barred from "the covenants of promise," but which Christ's death had abolished, giving Gentiles as well as Jews access to God. If one is looking for a text about social barriers, one can find it in Colossians 3:11 (without a parallel here in Ephesians) and in the texts that lie behind it in Galatians 3:28 and First Corinthians 12:12-13.

● In the second place, the interpretation of Ephesians is greatly facilitated when one pays attention to the parallel material in Colossians, with which our author seems to be acquainted. It is not the point of this comparison to be able to "chain link" references in a way that harmonizes passages. Rather, such a comparison helps the interpreter see more clearly the *distinctive* interests and ideas of each writer. The usefulness of this comparative approach will be further illustrated as we turn to the examination of a second passage from Ephesians.

Ephesians 5:21-33. When Ephesians 4:1 appeals to the readers in the name of Paul "to lead a life worthy of the calling to which [they] have been called," that calling is thought of largely in terms of the unity of all things, which for the author is the hallmark of God's plan for salvation, of Christ's sovereign lordship, and therefore of Christ's Body, the church. This is clear from the fact that the writer proceeds at once to urge the readers to be "eager to maintain the unity of the Spirit in the bond of peace," because "there is one body and one Spirit" (etc., 4:3-6). It is apparent, then, that the unity of all things in Christ, the overarching theme of chapters 1–3, continues to be emphasized in the exhortations of 4:1–6:20. These may be generally described as clustering around five major appeals: Grow up into Christ, 4:1-16 (see v 14); put off the old nature and put on the new, 4:17–5:2 (see 4:22-24); do not be deceived into doing evil, 5:3-20 (see v 6); be subject to one another, 5:23–6:9 (see 5:21); put on the whole armor of God, 6:10-20 (see v 11).

● Various alternative groupings of and headings for the exhortations in Ephesians 4:1–6:20 could be defended, but those above are probably as helpful as any, and perhaps more helpful than most. Notice how the attempt has been made to characterize the material in words drawn from the text itself. Of course, one must be prepared to revise one's preliminary judgments about a passage after it has been subjected to closer analysis.

Our specific passage opens what we have identified as the fourth main collection of appeals. In fact, the exhortation of 5:21 to "be subject to one another out of reverence for Christ" formulates in an inclusive way and effectively introduces the individual counsels that follow: to wives (5:22-24), husbands (5:23-33), children (6:1-3), fathers (6:4), slaves (6:5-8), and masters (6:9). These counsels, taken together, constitute a list that scholars, adopting Martin Luther's term, have often called a *Haustafel,* or "table of household duties," because its instructions are addressed in turn to the several groups that made up the ancient household. There are parallel passages, not only in Colossians 3:18–4:1, but also in First Peter 2:13–3:7 and, less clearly, in Titus 2:1-10. This seems to indicate that here we are in touch with a more or less standardized domestic code widely known and commended in Christian circles.

• Whether this code originated in Christian circles (perhaps developing from such Pauline passages as 1 Cor, chap 7 [esp. vv 17-24], and Rom 13:1-7) or is a Christian adaptation from some non-Christian (perhaps Stoic) source is disputed. A number of books and articles and all the best commentaries discuss this and related matters. The interpreter should recognize that when a passage is as closely paralleled in other New Testament writings as this one is, commentaries and articles on those passages, too, may be consulted for help.

One may suppose that Ephesians 5:21-33 stands in the church's lectionary principally because of the remarks about the relationship of Christ to his church in verses 23-27, 29-30, and 32. The real topic of the passage, however, concerns the relationship that should exist between husband and wife, as both the narrower (5:21–6:9) and broader (4:1–6:20) contexts require us to presume. This does not mean that the remarks about Christ and the church are *beside the point* of the appeals in which they are situated, but only that they are not the *main* point. This passage therefore presents two special challenges to interpreters: first, to discern how these two topics are at once distinct and related; and second, to consider in what respects, if any, these counsels may have meaning for Christians today. Naturally, the questions interpreters face in dealing with any biblical passage are present here as well, including questions about its situational context, the author's intentions, and the meaning of specific terms and concepts.

It is not possible to deal with all these questions and issues here. Certain general points can be registered, however, which may help to show how one might approach texts which, like the present one, contain rather specific directives for the Christian life.

One should begin by trying to distill the essence of the appeals themselves. This is especially important because the advice to wives and husbands has been so greatly expanded by comments about Christ and the church. (Note the much briefer treatments of the other relationships addressed in this code [6:1-9], and of the relationship between husbands and wives in the parallel codes [Col 3:18-19; 1 Pet 3:1-7; cf. Titus 2:2-4].) Wives are urged to "be subject" to their husbands (vv 22, 24) and husbands are admonished to "love" their wives (vv 25, 28), thus repeating the instructions in Colossians 3:18, 19 respectively, and almost duplicating those in First Peter 3:1 (despite RSV, the verb is again "to be subject") and 3:7 (where "love" is not used). That a wife was to be in all ways subordinate to her husband was commonly presupposed in most ancient, as in many modern cultures, and was undergirded by Roman law which vested specific rights and responsibilities in the male head of the household (the *pater familias*). In this respect, these codes reflect the contemporary cultural situation.

> ● In dealing with passages such as the one before us, interpreters need to take full account of the social context presupposed by the ancient writer and readers. One mark of a good commentary is its usefulness in describing that context. What would have struck a non-Christian most about the codes in their Christian formulation is the equal emphasis upon the husband's responsibility to "love" and care for the wife and, perhaps even more, the way the injunctions to each are theologically grounded.

The theological grounding of the whole hortatory section of Ephesians is apparent from the opening words in chapter 4, as we have seen. It is also clear from the words that introduce this code specifically ("out of reverence for Christ," 5:21) and from the christological references interposed throughout verses 22-33. These references and similar ones in the forms of the code that appear elsewhere in the New Testament function, in the first instance, to support the mutual relationship of subordination and love commended in the code. Here in Ephesians, the author's interest in Christ's relationship to the church has given the christological sanctions a special character and particularly illumines the form the writer believes a husband's love for his wife should take: Provide for both her material and spiritual needs (see esp. Eph 5:28-31, in which a text from Genesis is also employed). The love and nurture called for here is but a special form of that same loving, caring devotion to one another to which every believer had been called in Ephesians 5:1-2—where, as here, Christ's own self-giving love had been cited in order to sanction the appeal.

But what about the instructions to wives which we find in this and the other New Testament codes? What form is their subordination to their husbands to take?

This author, again elaborating on the brief instructions in Colossians 3:18-19, understands the wife's subordination to her husband as analogous to the church's subordination to Christ, meaning that it should be "in everything" (Eph 5:24) and that it should involve "respect" for the husband (v 33), even as the church honors Christ as its "head" and "Savior" (v 23). The concept of the man as the "head" of the woman is present in one of Paul's own letters (1 Cor 11:3), where the Apostle seems to connect it with the story of the creation of a woman from the first man's rib (Gen 2:21-23), to which he alludes in 11:8. In that context, then, "head" may have meant primarily "source," as it sometimes does in other places, so the emphasis would have been on woman's *dependence on* man more than on man's *rule over* woman.

> ● The interpreter should not presume that the meaning of man's "headship" in Ephesians 5 is identical with its meaning in First Corinthians 11, even if this later writer derived the image specifically from Paul (which is possible, but not necessary; the concept was probably widespread). Nevertheless, that and any other earlier (or contemporary) use of the imagery may help to shed light on what it meant to the author of Ephesians and what it would have meant to the readers.

Indeed Paul had modified even that point by observing that "man is now born of woman," so that their relationship is actually one of *interdependence,* especially since they are both ultimately *de*pendent on God alone (1 Cor 11:11-12).

This emphasis on the mutuality appropriate to the relationship between a man and a woman—which we have noted also in First Corinthians 7—is not quite so evident in Ephesians 5:22-33. But it is still present, implicitly at least, when Genesis 2:24 is quoted in verse 31 and when the two central admonitions of the passage are linked in verse 33. Moreover, one should not forget that here in Ephesians the whole domestic code has been introduced by the instruction to "be subject *to one another*" (5:21). This suggests that our author understands each of the specific instructions to be supportive of that general principle.

There is no unanimity among scholars concerning the specific functions these domestic codes served in the early church. One thing is certain, however—they are found only in writings from postapostolic times. They represent one of the ways the church of the late first and early second centuries sought to cope with the fact of Christ's delayed return. In these codes Christians were given advice on how they should conduct themselves within various social institutions. Paul had presumed that those institutions were "passing away" (1 Cor 7:31), but by the time of the Deutero-Pauline writers it had become clear that no matter what the long-term truth might be, for as long as anybody could now see, Christ's church must find a place within the structures and institutions of this world. Christian people must learn how to be faithful to the gospel in the midst of ongoing social responsibilities, such as being wives, husbands, children, parents, slaves, and masters.

In a way, then, the presence of these codes in the Deutero-Paulines is due no less to the church's eschatological outlook than is the absence of them from Paul's letters. It is just that the eschatological outlook has now changed. The stance of these codes toward the world is, in certain ways, a "conservative" one, for they presuppose only the need for Christians to get along in society, not the need for the social institutions themselves to be transformed. In another way, however, these codes help to sow the seeds of a Christian social ethic, insofar as they address themselves to the matter of living a responsible Christian life in society. The long-term importance of these codes, and of similar moral counsels in the later New Testament writings, lies not in what they taught about marriage, parenthood, or other specific topics. The interpreter must recognize that the *more* relevant specific moral teachings were for first- and second-century believers, the *less* specifically relevant they are apt to be for Christians of the twentieth century. Rather, their importance inheres in what they represent—the attempts of Christian people to relate their faith to their everyday conduct—and in how they seek to apply fundamental Christian convictions about the new life given in Christ to a new way of living in this world.

The Pastoral Epistles

It was probably some time in the first quarter of the second century that an anonymous writer composed the three documents that have come to be known as the Pastoral Epistles. The name is appropriate insofar as they contain advice allegedly given by Paul to Timothy and Titus, known to us from the Apostle's own letters as close and trusted associates in ministry. Moreover, this advice is communicated in a form modeled on the familiar Pauline letter. However, the traditional description is misleading insofar as it suggests that the chief concern of the letters is to define the tasks and qualifications of Christian pastors. That is involved, certainly, but the more basic objective of First and Second Timothy and of Titus is to invoke the authority of Paul and the whole Pauline tradition to combat a false teaching abroad in the churches with which this writer is acquainted (probably in western Asia Minor and on the island of Crete). This false teaching seems to have been some form of Christian Gnosticism (note the reference in 1 Tim 6:20 to "what is falsely called knowledge [*gnosis*]"), and warnings and admonitions about it are prominent in all three letters (see esp. 1 Tim 1:3-20; 2 Tim 1:6–3:9; Titus 2:1–3:11).

> ● Failure to be clear about this overall purpose can lead to grotesque misinterpretations and misapplications of texts from these writings. It is quite wrong, for instance, to regard such passages as First Timothy 1:4-7 as a condemnation of all theological inquiry and of all attempts to think clearly about the meaning of Christian faith. The "speculations" and "vain discussion" being criticized here are associated specifically with the esoteric doctrines of Gnostic teachers (their "myths and endless genealogies," v 4). Similarly, the arresting declaration of First Timothy 2:15 that "woman will be saved through bearing children" should probably be understood as a reaction to the view that marriage, sex, and childbearing are incompatible with the Christian life (see, e.g., 1 Tim 4:3). It certainly has no special relevance for modern discussions about contraception and abortion.

Whereas the other Deutero-Pauline writers were primarily concerned with interpreting, defending, and applying certain teachings of the Pauline tradition (in 2 Thess, Christ's return; in Col, Christ's cosmic lordship; in Eph, the unity of the church under Christ, its head), the author of the Pastorals is equally, or perhaps even more concerned with commending Paul himself. It is clear from the repetition of the formula in First Timothy 2:7 and Second Timothy 1:11 that this writer wants his readers to think of Paul as the church's great "preacher," "apostle," and "teacher"—an interesting sequence, since Paul himself certainly would have put the term *apostle* in first place.

But it is also clear that Paul is to be thought of as the great martyr and that the author wants these letters, or at least Second Timothy, to be regarded as Paul's "passing on the torch" to those who will continue his ministry. Time and again, therefore, this writer has "Paul" remind us of who he was and what he accomplished (note esp. 1 Tim 1:12-17; 2:7; 2 Tim 1:8-18; 3:10-13) and of the martyr's death, which was his destiny (2 Tim 2:8-13; 4:6-8). From this it follows that the readers of these letters (represented by "Timothy" and "Titus") are repeatedly charged to become the guardians of the apostolic tradition (see 1 Tim 1:2-4, 18-19; 4:6, 11-16; 6:2c-5, 11-16, 20; 2 Tim 1:13-14; 2:1-2, 8; 3:14; Titus 2:2, 15), a tradition this writer identifies with the Pauline gospel (1 Tim 1:10-11).

> • It is impossible to establish with any certainty the order in which First and Second Timothy and Titus were written, or at what intervals. The same issues seem to be in view in each, however, so the larger literary context of any given passage may be regarded with some confidence as the three taken together. While Timothy is portrayed as receiving the letters addressed to him in Ephesus (1 Tim 1:3-4; 2 Tim 1:16, 18, taken together with 4:19) and Titus is ostensibly in Crete (Titus 1:5), there is really not much to distinguish one letter from another.

A few comments on two representative passages will help to show some of the matters to which an interpreter of the Pastoral Epistles must be attentive.

First Timothy 1:3-11. After the salutation (1:1-2) this author moves straight to the body of his letter, omitting the paragraph of thanksgiving which stands in most of the other letters in the Pauline corpus. The letter body consists mainly of instructions about "how one ought to behave in the household of God" (1 Tim 2:1–6:2*b*; see 3:15), but these must all be read in light of the admonitions in 1:3-20 to oppose false teachings. It is the activity of "certain persons" teaching a doctrine "different" from Paul's (1:3) that has prompted the writing of First Timothy and caused its author to set forth his understanding of the way Pauline congregations should conduct themselves. The admonitions of 1:3-20 consist of Paul's charge to Timothy about the errant teaching (1:3-7), some counsel about the role of the Law (1:8-11), a reminder that Paul had been commissioned to apostleship by reason of God's grace (1:12-17), and a reiteration of the charge to Timothy (1:18-20).

It is in the original statement of the charge (1:3-7) that we are introduced to the problem with which all three of these Pastoral Epistles are more or less preoccupied. The false teachers are not named here, although "Hymenaeus and Alexander" are mentioned in 1:20 as being two of them.

> • One of the perplexing things about the Pastorals is the appearance of so many names and various particulars about Paul's activities (see also, e.g., 2 Tim 1:5, 15-18; 4:9-18, 19-21; Titus 3:12-13). Were Hymenaeus (also mentioned in 2 Tim 2:17) and Alexander ("the coppersmith" of 2 Tim 4:14) known to have opposed Paul during his lifetime? Or were they invented by this author to give his "letter from Paul" greater verisimilitude? Such questions have no clear answers, and even if they did, it is doubtful whether the interpreter would be in a much better position than at present to understand the author's concerns and perspectives.

Their "different doctrine" involves, in our writer's view, highly speculative and ultimately meaningless discussions about "myths and endless genealogies." The reference in

Titus 1:14 to "*Jewish* myths" may suggest that a gnosticizing type of Judaism is being discussed. If so, one could better understand the comment here in First Timothy that the errant Christians are "desiring to be teachers of the law" (1:7).

> ● While not much is said in First Timothy 1:3-7 about the false teaching, there are sufficient clues provided to start the interpreter on a hunt through all the Pastorals for further information. The reference to "Jewish myths" in Titus is but one example; there are additional clues (in 1 Tim 1:19-20; 4:7; 6:4-5, 20; and 2 Tim and Titus). In dealing with this kind of issue, however, it is imperative that the interpreter look beyond the New Testament itself to first- and second-century texts which reveal more about heterodox forms of Christianity in the period. A study by Dennis Ronald MacDonald does this very well, with some interesting results.[1]

Our author's derogatory reference to "teachers of the law" prompts him to comment in verses 8-11 on the extent to which "the law is good." Its proper function, we are told, is to restrain wrongdoers from the kinds of vices enumerated in verses 9-10. How far this idea is from Paul's own conception of the role of the Law can be seen by comparing such passages as Romans 7:7-12, in which the Apostle insisted that Law is the means by which sin gains entry into one's life and is thus exposed as sin. This shows that for Paul, the Law had not been given only "for the lawless and disobedient," as our author now insists (v 9), but in order that all people might discover themselves to be sinners who have fallen short of the glory of God (cf. Rom 3:21-23). Moreover, for

---

[1] *The Legend and the Apostle: The Battle for Paul in Story and Canon* (Philadelphia: Westminster Press, 1983).

Paul himself, Christ represented "the end of the law" (Rom 10:4; cf. Gal 3:23-25).

How should one deal with this discrepancy between Paul and his interpreter? The difference is too fundamental to warrant our describing First Timothy 1:8-11 as merely a supplement to or a modification of the Apostle's own teaching. Are we to conclude, then, that the author of the Pastorals has simply misrepresented Paul, either intentionally or because he misunderstood him?

On the one hand, we must acknowledge that this later writer does not make the kind of seminal contributions that Paul makes to our understanding of the gospel and its meaning. On the other hand, we must also recognize that the issues with which Paul dealt (Are Gentiles excluded in principle from the Law's promise of life? Is that promise fulfilled by one's adherence to its Commandments?) are not the issues facing the author of the Pastorals. This is exhibited especially well by Second Timothy 1:9 and Titus 3:5. There the Pauline idea that salvation comes as a gift is strongly affirmed, but set over against it is the idea that salvation comes "by works"; Paul would have said, "by works *of (the) law*" (Rom 3:28; Gal 2:16, etc.). The only specific references to the Law here in the Pastorals are in the passage before us (1 Tim 1:7, 8, 9) and in Titus 3:9 ("quarrels over the law"). The false teachers were evidently calling upon the Law to support their strange doctrines. Now, in opposition to them, our author insists that its only "lawful" use is for moral guidance and discipline, something he thinks the predominantly Gentile church of his day badly needs.

● Modern readers will have no difficulty understanding this conception of the Law's proper role and function. It is Paul's own much more complex understanding of the Law that will give them trouble. Precisely for this reason it is important to be as clear as possible about the differences between the two. Each view must be understood in accord with its own theological and situational contexts.

Second Timothy 3:10–4:8. More specifically and pervasively than the other Pastorals, Second Timothy presents Paul as the martyr-Apostle. Thus his imprisonment and suffering are in view from the very first chapter (see 1:8, 12, 16), and his portrayal as a courageous "soldier" for the faith (2:3-4; 4:7) lends force to that theme. It seems clear that the author wants us to regard Second Timothy as Paul's last letter to Timothy, written not long before the Apostle's death. For this reason the contents of the letter body, which runs from 1:6 through 4:8, have a special character. The appeals in 2:8–3:9 to avoid the false teachers and their doctrines are preceded by several paragraphs emphasizing the importance of guarding the truth, entrusted first to Paul, then to his immediate followers, and subsequently to the following generations (see 1:12*b*, 14; 2:2). Indeed, this first section of the letter body opens with a reminder that Paul's follower has been commissioned by the Apostle to help guarantee that tradition (1:6-7).

> • The interpreter will observe that some English versions (in addition to the RSV, see the New International Version and Today's English Version) include 1:6-7 as part of the paragraph that begins in verse 3. It is better, however, to regard 1:3-5 as the standard paragraph of thanksgiving and therefore as a part of the letter opening, and to connect 1:6-7 with the verses that follow, as do The Jerusalem Bible, The New English Bible, and The New American Bible. The appeal in verses 6-7 marks the opening of the letter body.

The passage before us, Second Timothy 3:10–4:8, constitutes the second section of the letter body. It is essentially a commendation of the example of Paul's life and teaching (see 3:10-14) and a charge to carry on Paul's ministry, since the Apostle himself has now "finished the race" (4:1-8). It is especially important to recognize this basic function of the passage, since many readers are distracted from it by the comments in 3:15-16 about Scripture. The passage as such is not "about" Scripture, even though the verses in question are important ones. Actually, what is most interesting here is the author's concern with tracing Timothy's religious heritage to *both* Paul and Scripture (3:14-15). Does this author in fact presume, as the author of Second Peter certainly does—probably several decades later (2 Pet 3:16)—that the Apostle's letters are to be regarded along with the Old Testament as "sacred writings"? If so, we see here one important benchmark in the emergence of a New Testament canon. But even if the author does not reckon the Pauline letters as scriptural, it is important to notice that the Pauline tradition is being called on *along with* Scripture as the church marshals its forces to combat errant teaching.

While one may grant readily enough that the comments about Scripture in 3:15-16 are secondary to the main point of the passage, that is no reason to pass over them lightly. The fact remains that interpreters of the Bible often appeal to them as proof that this writer (whether Paul or not) regarded Scripture (perhaps including his own writings) as being without substantial error and, moreover (v 17), as providing all the guidance one needs in matters of Christian faith and practice. There are at least two problems with this inter-pretation, quite apart from the uncertainty as to which writings specifically are included in the author's notion of "scripture."

First, there is a question about the best way to translate verse 16. The Revised Standard Version, for example, offers two different renderings, one in the body of the text and one in a footnote.

> ● There are various instances like this throughout the Revised Standard Version and other versions of the Bible. The interpreter should pay close attention to these alternative translations. Moreover, when such a footnote is encountered—say in the Revised Standard Version—it should prompt the reader to consult other versions for their renderings.

The main translation reads, "All scripture is inspired by God and profitable for teaching," while the alternative given is, "Every scripture inspired by God is also profitable for teaching." There is an important difference in emphasis here. In the first, the writer is understood to emphasize that "all scripture is inspired by God," whereas in the second, he is understood to emphasize that Scripture, as contrasted with profane writings, "is also profitable for teaching."

Today's English Version and The Jerusalem Bible, like the Revised Standard Version, give readers a choice of these two understandings. The New International Version and The New American Bible provide only the first, while The New English Bible provides only the second. How, then, is the interpreter to make a decision in the matter? In such a case it is imperative to consult the commentaries and other special aids, including the Greek text if one is able. While the commentators themselves do not agree on which understanding is best, they will at least give some indication why they think one is preferable to the other.

In our view the context supports the rendering offered in the Revised Standard Version footnote. The point in the preceding verse (2 Tim 3:15) is that Scripture, called "the sacred writings," is "able to instruct you for salvation through faith in Christ Jesus"—that is, it proclaims the gospel. The most natural way to read verse 16 is as an extension of this point. Now we are told that Scripture "is also profitable for teaching," and so on—that is, it also provides "training in righteousness." Thus the phrase "inspired by God" is a description of "scripture" (parallel to "the sacred writings" in v 15) and not the predicate of an independent clause. The inspiration of Scripture is presumed, but no specific theory of inspiration is proposed.

Second, it is quite gratuitous to presume that "inspired by God" necessarily means that this author would subscribe to the notion of the verbal inerrancy of Scripture as that doctrine developed, particularly in the nineteenth and twentieth centuries. "Inspired" translates a term that means literally *God-breathed* and is applicable, literally, only to an animate being. Here, where it has been applied metaphorically to Scripture, an inanimate object, we can say only that the intention is to identify that object as in some special way graced by God's own presence. Not only is there no theory of inspiration here; there is also no attempt whatever to draw conclusions about the inerrancy of Scripture.

● It is instructive to contrast Second Peter 1:20-21 with Second Timothy 3:15-16. That later writer comes closer to a theory of inspiration when he writes that "no prophecy ever came by the impulse of man, but men moved by the Holy Spirit spoke from God" (2 Pet 1:21). Furthermore, in Second Peter the issue is very specifically the *interpretation* of Scripture: "First of all you must understand this, that no prophecy of scripture is a matter of one's own interpretation" (2 Pet 1:20). This is written in opposition to people who do not subscribe to the writer's own belief in the literal truth of scriptural prophecies about the Lord's return (see 2 Pet 3:3-4). His response to them is that those prophecies must be taken at face value because they derive ultimately from God.

In Second Timothy, however, it is not the author's primary
concern to defend a particular view of the origin of Scripture
or of how it should be interpreted. His concern is to
commend Scripture, along with the Pauline gospel, as
constituting the fundamentals of the church's faith and life.

Finally, then, one must return to a consideration of the
main function of the passage in which these comments about
Scripture occur—Second Timothy 3:10–4:8. In this last
major section of the letter, Paul's teaching is once more
commended (3:10, 14), and Timothy is once more urged to
carry on the Apostle's work (4:1-2, 5). There is, however, no
attempt to summarize the content of Paul's teaching.
Instead, there is a recapitulation of Paul's life—we are
reminded of his "faith . . . patience . . . love . . .
steadfastness . . . persecutions . . . [and] sufferings" (3:10-
11). His martyrdom also comes into view here (4:6), and
even his coronation with final righteousness by the exalted
Lord (4:8). This is the way the author of the Pastoral Epistles
wanted the church to remember its Apostle.

AIDS FOR THE INTERPRETER

General Works

Interpreters of the Pauline literature will want to consult several different English versions as they work, and a good recent discussion of these may be found in *The Word of God: A Guide to English Versions of the Bible,* edited by Lloyd R. Bailey (Atlanta: John Knox Press, 1982). In addition to the translations, another basic tool is Clinton Morrison's *Analytical Concordance to the Revised Standard Version of the New Testament* (Philadelphia: Westminster Press, 1979). The book by John H. Hayes and Carl R. Holladay, *Biblical Exegesis: A Beginner's Handbook* (Atlanta: John Knox Press, 1982), may be commended not only to those who need an introduction to exegetical work, but also to those who need to review what exegesis involves. The five-volume *Interpreter's Dictionary of the Bible,* edited by George A. Buttrick, K. Crim, and others (Nashville: Abingdon Press, 1962 [vols. 1–4]; 1976 [suppl. vol.]), and the revised edition of the four-volume *International Standard Bible Encyclopedia,* edited by G. W. Bromiley and others (Grand Rapids:

Eerdmans Publishing Co., 1979 and following), contain many excellent articles on people, places, themes, and issues pertinent to one's study of the Pauline letters.

Ready access to comprehensive books on Paul is essential for interpreting either the lifework of the Apostle or particular passages. As pointed out in chapter 1, one's interpretation of Paul depends on the range of texts one considers Pauline and on how one regards Acts. The most recent major book which fits the Pauline letters into the framework of Acts is F. F. Bruce, *Paul: Apostle of the Heart Set Free* (Grand Rapids: Eerdmans Publishing Co., 1979); the most recent treatment which includes the Deutero-Pauline letters is Herman Ridderbos, *Paul: An Outline of His Theology* (Grand Rapids: Eerdmans Publishing Co., 1975). On the other hand, the best overall presentation, one which first reconstructs Paul's career and then summarizes his thought on the basis of the undisputed letters, is Günther Bornkamm, *Paul* (New York: Harper & Row, 1971). For a convenient presentation of Paul's thought, distinguishing between what Paul shared with the early church and what he found necessary to defend and interpret, see Leander E. Keck, *Paul and His Letters* (Philadelphia: Fortress Press, 1979). A major interpretation of Paul's theology which emphasizes its apocalyptic cast is J. Christiaan Beker, *Paul: The Triumph of God in Life and Thought* (Philadelphia: Fortress Press, 1980). The best discussion of the Pauline letters from a Structuralist perspective, yet free of jargon, is Daniel Patte, *Paul's Faith and the Power of the Gospel* (Philadelphia: Fortress Press, 1983).

Commentaries

We judge the following commentaries on the several letters of the Pauline corpus to be among the best currently available in English. Some are more and some are less technical and thorough, but each is worth consulting.

Romans

C. K. Barrett, *A Commentary on the Epistle to the Romans,* Harper's New Testament Commentaries (New York: Harper & Row, 1957). A solid, concise treatment, with the author's own translation; Greek not required.

C.E.B. Cranfield, *A Critical and Exegetical Commentary on the Epistle to the Romans,* International Critical Commentary, 2 vols. (Edinburgh: T. & T. Clark, 1975, 1979). This work, based on the Greek text, lays out the options and gives steady attention to the history of exegesis.

Ernst Käsemann, *Commentary on Romans* (Grand Rapids: Eerdmans Publishing Co., 1980). The most important interpretation of Paul since Barth and Bultmann; repays study, but not easy to read.

First Corinthians

C. K. Barrett, *The First Epistle to the Corinthians,* Harper's New Testament Commentaries (New York: Harper & Row, 1968). A solid, concise treatment, with the author's own translation; Greek not required.

Second Corinthians

C. K. Barrett, *The Second Epistle to the Corinthians,* Harper's New Testament Commentaries (New York: Harper & Row, 1973). A solid, concise treatment, with the author's own translation; Greek not required.

Victor Paul Furnish, *II Corinthians,* Anchor Bible 32A (Garden City, N.Y.: Doubleday & Co., 1984). A detailed treatment of the issues, with the author's own translation; Greek not required.

Galatians

Hans Dieter Betz, *Galatians,* Hermeneia (Philadelphia: Fortress Press, 1979). The best commentary in English, based on the Greek text; emphasizes Paul's use of rhetoric. Excellent for classical bibliography. A knowledge of Greek helpful, but not required.

Charles B. Cousar, *Galatians,* Interpretation (Atlanta: John Knox Press, 1982). A solid, concise commentary "for teaching and preaching"; Greek not required.

Ephesians

Markus Barth, *Ephesians,* 2 vols., Anchor Bible 34 and 34A (New York: Doubleday & Co., 1974). This lengthy exposition defends Pauline authorship; Greek not required.

C. Leslie Mitton, *Ephesians,* New Century Bible (Grand Rapids: Eerdmans Publishing Co., 1981). A brief exposition of Ephesians as a Deutero-Pauline writing; Greek not required.

Philippians

Frank W. Beare, *A Commentary on the Epistle to the Philippians,* Harper's New Testament Commentaries (New York: Harper & Row, 1959). A solid, concise treatment, with the author's own translation; Greek not required.

Colossians and Philemon

Eduard Lohse, *Colossians and Philemon,* Hermeneia (Philadelphia: Fortress Press, 1971). The best commentary in English on these two letters; regards Colossians as Deutero-Pauline. A knowledge of Greek helpful, but not required.

Peter T. O'Brien, *Colossians, Philemon,* Word Biblical Commentary 44 (Waco, Tex.: Word Books, 1982). The apostolic authorship of Colossians is defended; comments are based on the Greek text, with the author's own translation provided.

Eduard Schweizer, *The Letter to the Colossians: A Commentary* (Minneapolis: Augsburg Publishing House, 1982). Less technical than the commentaries by Lohse and O'Brien. This author favors the view that Timothy had some hand in the composition of Colossians; Greek not required.

First and Second Thessalonians

Ernest Best, *The First and Second Epistles to the Thessalonians,* Black's New Testament Commentaries (London: Adam & Charles Black, 1972). This commentary, unfortunately, is no longer available in an American edition. The Pauline authorship of Second Thessalonians is defended, but somewhat tentatively; Greek not required.

The Pastoral Epistles

Martin Dibelius and Hans Conzelmann, *The Pastoral Epistles,* Hermeneia (Philadelphia: Fortress Press, 1972). Dibelius' commentary, first published in German in 1913 and revised by Conzelmann in 1953 and 1966, is a classic. A knowledge of Greek helpful, but not required.

Anthony T. Hanson, *The Pastoral Epistles,* New Century Bible (Grand Rapids: Eerdmans Publishing Co., 1982). An excellent treatment, although brief; Greek not required.

Special Studies

Victor Paul Furnish, *The Moral Teaching of Paul: Selected Issues* (Nashville: Abingdon Press, 1979). A concise, nontechnical treatment of particular topics such as sex, homosexuality, women in the church, and political power.

————, *Theology and Ethics in Paul* (Nashville: Abingdon Press, 1968). A thorough treatment of the subject.

Ernst Käsemann, *New Testament Questions of Today* (Philadelphia: Fortress Press, 1969). Contains six essays on Paul, including " 'The Righteousness of God' in Paul," a turning point in recent interpretation of Paul.

————, *Perspectives on Paul* (Philadelphia: Fortress Press, 1971). Seven penetrating essays which deserve careful reading.

Wayne A. Meeks, *The First Urban Christians* (New Haven: Yale University Press, 1983). The first major comprehensive study of the Pauline churches from a sociological perspective.

E. P. Sanders, *Paul and Palestinian Judaism* (Philadelphia: Fortress Press, 1977). The most important recent attempt to interpret Paul in light of the patterning of thought among rabbis, Dead Sea Scrolls, and Apocrypha and Pseudepigrapha, respectively.